Construction OSHA Compliance Handbook

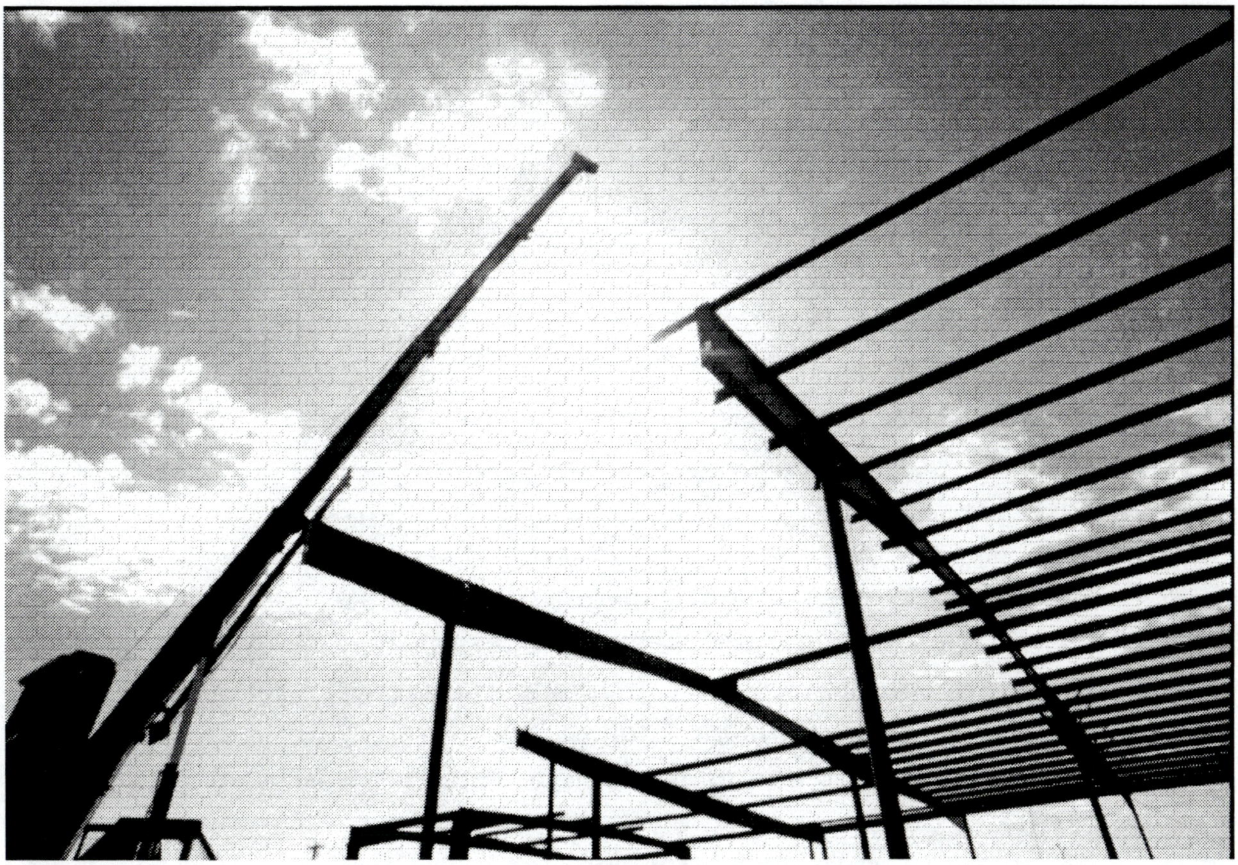

January 2001

J. J. Keller
& Associates, Inc.

© 2001

J. J. Keller & Associates, Inc.
3003 W. Breezewood Lane - P. O. Box 368
Neenah, Wisconsin 54957-0368
Phone: (800) 327-6868
Fax: (800) 727-7516
www.jjkeller.com

United States laws and Federal regulations published as promulgated are in public domain. However, their compilation and arrangement along with other materials in this publication are subject to the copyright notice.

Library of Congress Catalog Card Number: 92-71326
ISBN 1-877798-08-8
Canadian Goods and Services Tax (GST) Number: R123-317687

All rights reserved. Neither the Handbook nor any part thereof may be reproduced in any manner without written permission of the Publisher.

Printed in the U.S.A.
Twelfth Edition, January 2001

KELLER CONSTRUCTION, UTILITY & MINE SAFETY COMPLIANCE PRODUCTS

Construction Regulatory Guide - 139G
Construction Safety and Health Compliance Manual - 139M
Construction Regulatory Update (Newsletter) - 3N
Construction Toolbox Talks - 75M
Official OSHA Construction Safety Handbook - 201ORS
OSHA Construction Safety Training Organizer - 201PSG
Keller-Soft Compliance Information Manager (CD-ROM) - 100KS
OSHA Workplace Safety (CD-ROM) - 34PDR
Forklift Safety for Construction - Video Training Kit - 226K
Utility Safety Handbook - 202ORS
MSHA Compliance Manual for Surface Operations - 77M
Fleet Safety Compliance Manual - 8M
Trucking Safety Guide - 8G

Introduction

This Construction OSHA Compliance Handbook is an aid to help you comply with OSHA regulations at your jobsites. It is a handy reference that is far more convenient to take along with you than the actual OSHA construction regulations.

The handbook does not contain all of the safety and health standards applicable to the construction industry. It does, however, contain an overview of those rules most frequently overlooked by construction employers (according to citation statistics) and those covering situations that are particularly hazardous.

The first section of the handbook, a list of the top 100 OSHA construction citations, summarizes the Part 1926 OSHA rules that are most frequently cited by OSHA inspectors at construction jobsites. A review of this list, along with prompt corrective action, can help you eliminate these common hazards and possibly avert an OSHA citation.

The next three sections provide an overview of the key OSHA standards that apply to construction. The rules summarized in these sections are found in 29 CFR (Code of Federal Regulations) Part 1926, the construction safety and health regulations; Part 1910, the general industry standards; Part 1903, inspections, citations, and penalties; and Part 1904, recording and reporting injuries and illnesses.

The final three sections, OSHA Special Emphasis & Focused Programs, Other OSHA Special Interest Areas, and Related Regulations for Construction, give you an overview of OSHA construction programs, and other agency regulations that you won't find in the construction standards but should be aware of. Other agency regulations include such requirements as the Americans with Disabilities Act, EPA and asbestos, EPA's Community Right To Know, and the Army Corps of Engineer's wetlands program.

A key word index is included in the handbook to enable you to locate the correct OSHA regulation with minimal effort.

Due to the constantly changing nature of government regulations, it is impossible to guarantee absolute accuracy of the material contained herein. The Publisher and Editors, therefore, cannot assume any responsibility for omissions, errors, misprinting, or ambiguity contained within this publication and shall not be held liable in any degree for any loss or injury caused by such omission, error, misprinting or ambiguity presented in this publication.

This publication is designed to provide reasonably accurate and authoritative information in regard to the subject matter covered. It is sold with the understanding that the Publisher is not engaged in rendering legal, accounting, or other professional service. If legal advice or other expert assistance is required, the services of a competent professional person should be sought.

The Editors
J. J. Keller & Associates, Inc.

Table of Contents

	Page
Top 100 Most Frequently Cited OSHA Construction Regulations	7
Other related and frequently cited OSHA regulations	10
Summaries of the Most Frequently Cited and Other Key OSHA Construction Regulations	11
General safety and health provisions—§1926.20	11
Safety training and education—§1926.21	12
Housekeeping—§1926.25	12
Means of egress—§1926.34	12
Employee emergency action plans—§1926.35	13
Medical services and first aid—§1926.50	13
Sanitation—§1926.51	13
Occupational noise exposure—§1926.52	14
Nonionizing radiation (lasers)—§1926.54	15
Gases, vapors, fumes, dusts, and mists—§1926.55	15
Illumination—§1926.56	15
Hazard communication—§1910.1200	16
Lead—§1926.62	18
Personal protective equipment (PPE)—§1926, Subpart E	20
Fire protection—§1926.150	22
Fire prevention—§1926.151	22
Flammable and combustible liquids—§1926.152	22
Liquified petroleum gas—§1926.153	23
Temporary heating devices—§1926.154	24
Accident prevention signs and tags—§1926.200	24
Signaling—§1926.201	25
Materials storage—§1926.250	25
Rigging equipment for materials handling—§1926.251	26
Waste material disposal—§1926.252	27
Tools, hand and power—§1926, Subpart I	28
Welding and cutting—§1926, Subpart J	30
Electrical—§1926, Subpart K	32
Scaffolding—§1926, Subpart L	36
Fall protection—§1926, Subpart M	40
Cranes, derricks, hoists, elevators, and conveyors—§1926, Subpart N	46

	Page
Motor vehicles, mechanized equipment, and marine operations (including forklifts)—§1926, Subpart O	48
Excavations—§1926, Subpart P	50
Concrete and masonry construction—§1926, Subpart Q	54
Steel erection—§1926, Subpart R	54
Demolition—§1926, Subpart T	55
Stairways and ladders—§1926, Subpart X	55
Asbestos—§1926.1101	60

Summaries of Key OSHA General Industry (29 CFR Part 1910) Regulations Construction Companies are Frequently Cited for 65

Protection of open-sided floors, platforms, and runways—§1910.23(c)(1)	65
Vehicle-mounted elevating and rotating work platforms—Extensible and articulating boom platforms—§1910.67(c)(2)	65
Personal protective equipment—Application—§1910.132(a)	66
Personal protective equipment—Hazard assessment and equipment selection—§1910.132(d)(1)	66
Personal protective equipment—Eye and face protection—§1910.133(a)(1)	67
The control of hazardous energy (lockout/tagout)—§1910.147(c)(1), (4), (6), & (7)	67
Electrical—General requirements—§1910.303(g)(2)	67
Electrical—Wiring design & protection—§1910.304(f)(4)	68
Electrical—Identification, splices, and terminations—§1910.305(g)(2)	68
Electrical—Lockout and tagging—§1910.333(b)(2)	68

Other Requirements Frequently Cited 69

General Duty Clause—5(a)(1)	69
When can OSHA give you a General Duty Clause citation?	70
Inspections, citations and proposed penalties—Part 1903	70
Recording and reporting occupational injuries and illnesses—Part 1904	72

OSHA Special Emphasis and Focused Programs 77

Crystalline Silica—OSHA's Special Emphasis Program	77
Lead in Construction—OSHA's Special Emphasis Program	79
Trenching and Excavations—OSHA's Special Emphasis Program	82
OSHA's Focused Inspection Initiative for Construction Jobsites	84

Table of Contents

Page

Other OSHA Special Interest Areas 89
Residential Construction—OSHA's Interim Fall Protection Compliance Guidelines 89
Steel Erection—OSHA's Interim Fall Protection Compliance Guidelines 91
Communication Tower Construction Activities—Interim Inspection Procedures 93
Work Zone Safety 103
Ultraviolet Radiation 108
Heat and Cold Stress Equation 110

Related Regulations for Construction 117
Asbestos (EPA) 117
Lead (EPA) 118
Stormwater (EPA) 122
Wetlands (EPA) 125
Community Right to Know (EPA) 127
Hazardous Waste (EPA) 129
Americans with Disabilities Act (EEOC) 131
Fair Labor Standards Act—Child Labor Provisions (DOL) 133
Family and Medical Leave Act (DOL) 135
Employment Discrimination in Construction (DOL) 137
Wage, Hour and Fringe Benefit Standards for Construction Contracts (DOL) 139
Kickbacks in Federally Funded Construction (DOL) 141

Key Word Index 143

Top 100 Most Frequently Cited OSHA Construction Regulations

OSHA's major enforcement tool is the jobsite inspection. Inspections often result in the discovery of violations of OSHA standards.

As a construction company subject to OSHA inspections, it may be helpful for you to know what rules OSHA is citing most frequently. Knowing this information can help you determine if your workplace is in compliance—or may need improvements.

This section lists the 100 most frequently cited Federal OSHA Part 1926 construction standards (October 1, 1999 through September 30, 2000). These statistics only cover those states that fall under the jurisdiction of Federal OSHA. Those 21 states that have their own OSHA programs are not included.

	Section	Description	Total Violations
1	.451(g)(1)	Scaffolding—Fall protection	1796
2	.501(b)(1)	Fall protection—Unprotected sides and edges	1681
3	.100(a)	PPE—Head protection	1192
4	.652(a)(1)	Excavations—Protection of employees in excavations	987
5	.21(b)(2)	Safety training and education—Employer responsibility	920
6	.451(e)(1)	Scaffolding—Access	889
7	.451(b)(1)	Scaffolding—Platform construction—Planking	869
8	.404(b)(1)	Electrical—Ground-fault protection	789
9	.451(c)(2)	Scaffolding—Supported scaffolds—Base plates	753
10	.20(b)(2)	Accident prevention responsibilities—Jobsite inspections	728
11	.503(a)(1)	Fall protection—Training program	693
12	.1053(b)(1)	Ladders—Use—Three foot extension above upper landing	624
13	1910.1200(e)(1)	Hazard communication—Written hazard communication program	618
14	.453(b)(2)	Scaffolding—Aerial lifts—Extensible and articulating boom platforms	618
15	.501(b)(13)	Fall protection—Residential construction	618
16	.454(a)	Scaffolding—Training requirements	609
17	.20(b)(1)	Accident prevention responsibilities—Necessary programs	586
18	.501(b)(4)	Fall protection—Holes	558
19	.1052(c)(1)	Stairways—Stairrails and handrails	468
20	.651(c)(2)	Excavations—Access and egress	455
21	.501(b)(10)	Fall protection—Roofing work on low-slope roofs	438
22	.405(a)(2)	Electrical—Wiring methods—Temporary wiring	412

	Section	Description	Total Violations
23	.451(g)(4)	Scaffolding—Guardrail systems	412
24	.651(k)(1)	Excavations—Inspections	409
25	.451(f)(7)	Scaffolding—Erecting, dismantling, moving, and altering	377
26	.404(f)(6)	Electrical—Wiring design and protection—Grounding path	358
27	.102(a)(1)	PPE—Eye and face protection	349
28	.25(a)	Housekeeping	348
29	.701(b)	Concrete and masonry construction—Impalement hazards—Rebar	328
30	.651(j)(2)	Excavations—Loose rock or soil	324
31	.405(g)(2)	Electrical—Identification, splices, and terminations	291
32	.451(f)(3)	Scaffolding—Inspection	269
33	.501(b)(11)	Fall protection—Steep roofs	255
34	.150(c)(1)	Fire protection—Portable firefighting equipment	252
35	.501(b)(14)	Fall protection—Wall openings	246
36	.95(a)	PPE—Criteria for personal protective equipment	236
37	.452(c)(2)	Scaffolding—Fabricated frame scaffolds	222
38	1910.1200(h)(1)	Hazard communication—Employee information and training	220
39	1910.1200(g)(1)	Hazard communication—Material safety data sheets	218
40	1910.1200(h)	Hazard communication—Employee information and training	217
41	.1051(a)	Stairways and ladders—Personal points of access	205
42	.403(b)(2)	Electrical—Examination, installation, and use of equipment	204
43	.403(i)(2)	Electrical—Guarding electrical equipment live parts	204
44	1910.1200(g)(8)	Hazard communication—Material safety data sheets	191
45	.1060(a)	Stairways and ladders—Training requirements	180
46	.602(c)(1)	Material handling equipment—Lifting and hauling equipment	163
47	1910.134(c)(1)	Respiratory protection—Respiratory protection program	162
48	.1053(b)(4)	Ladders—Use only for purpose designed for	160
49	.62(d)(2)	Lead—Exposure assessment	159
50	.105(a)	PPE—Safety nets	159
51	.304(f)	Tools—Woodworking tools	159
52	.405(b)(2)	Electrical—Wiring methods, components, and equipment	155
53	.350(a)(9)	Gas welding and cutting—Gas cylinders	146
54	.454(b)	Scaffolding—Training requirements	144
55	.416(e)(1)	Electrical—Safety related work practices—Cords and cables	137
56	.501(b)(15)	Fall protection—Walking/working surfaces not otherwise addressed	137
57	.1053(b)(13)	Ladders—Top step	136

Top 100 Citations

	Section	Description	Total Violations
58	.28(a)	Personal protective equipment—Employer responsibility	131
59	.350(a)(10)	Welding and cutting—Storing gas cylinders	131
60	.451(c)(1)	Scaffolding—Criteria for supported scaffolds	130
61	.451(h)(2)	Scaffolding—Falling object protection	126
62	1910.134(e)(1)	Medical evaluation	125
63	.403(b)(1)	Electrical—Approved equipment	119
64	1910.134(d)(1)	Respiratory protection—Selection of respirators	116
65	.602(a)(9)	Material handling equipment—Earthmoving equipment	115
66	.651(k)(2)	Excavations—Inspections	113
67	.503(b)(1)	Fall protection—Certification of training	112
68	.503(c)	Fall protection—Retraining	109
69	.405(b)(1)	Wiring methods—Cabinets, boxes, and fittings	108
70	.451(b)(2)	Scaffolding—Platform construction	108
71	.62(d)(1)	Lead—Exposure assessment	106
72	.503(a)(2)	Fall protection—Training program	102
73	.451(b)(5)	Scaffolding—Platform construction	100
74	.416(a)(1)	Electrical—Protection of employees	96
75	.1052(c)(12)	Stairways—Guardrails	96
76	.451(f)(4)	Scaffolding—Damaged or weakened	93
77	.403(h)	Electrical—Identification of disconnecting means and circuits	92
78	.451(h)(1)	Scaffolding—Falling object protection	90
79	.1053(b)(16)	Ladders—Structural defects	90
80	.1053(b)(8)	Ladders—Securing ladders	86
81	1910.1200(f)(5)	Hazard communication—Labels and other forms of warning	84
82	.501(b)(2)	Fall protection—Leading edges	84
83	.502(i)(3)	Fall protection—Covers	82
84	.50(c)	Medical services and first aid	80
85	.405(g)(1)	Electrical—Wiring methods, components, equipment for general use	80
86	.501(b)(3)	Fall protection—Hoist areas	79
87	.405(j)(1)	Electrical—Wiring methods, components, equipment for general use	77
88	.451(c)(3)	Scaffolding—Criteria for supported scaffolds—Poles, legs, and uprights	76
89	.502(b)(1)	Fall protection systems—Guardrail systems	76
90	.300(b)(1)	Tools, hand and power—Guarding	75
91	.152(a)(1)	Flammable and combustible liquids—General requirements	74
92	.1053(b)(6)	Ladders—Use	71

- 9 -

	Section	Description	Total Violations
93	.452(w)(2)	Scaffolding—Mobile scaffolds	70
94	.502(b)(2)	Fall protection systems—Guardrail systems	70
95	.550(b)(2)	Cranes and derricks—Crawler, locomotive, and truck cranes	67
96	.300(b)(2)	Tools, hand and power—Guarding	66
97	.1052(b)(1)	Stairways—Temporary service	66
98	.452(c)(4)	Scaffolds—Fabricated frame scaffolds	66
99	.1101(g)(1)	Asbestos—Methods of compliance	65
100	.651(d)	Excavations—Exposure to vehicular traffic	64

Other related and frequently cited OSHA regulations

Section	Description	Total Violations
5(a)(1)	General Duty Clause of the OSH Act	319
1904.2(a)	Recording and reporting occupational injuries and illnesses—Log and summary of occupational injuries and illnesses	64
1903.19(c)(1)	Inspections, citations and proposed penalties—Abatement verification—Certification	53
1904.8	Recording and reporting occupational injuries and illnesses—Reporting of fatality or multiple hospitalization incidents	43
1904.7	Recording and reporting occupational injuries and illnesses—Access to records	12
1903.19(d)(1)	Inspections, citations and proposed penalties—Abatement verification—Documentation	8
1904.5(a)	Recording and reporting occupational injuries and illnesses—Annual summary	4
1904.4	Recording and reporting occupational injuries and illnesses—Supplementary record	4

Summaries of the Most Frequently Cited and Other Key OSHA Construction Regulations

OSHA regulations specifically applying to the construction industry are found in 29 CFR Part 1926. Many of those requirements are summarized in this section. The standards summarized represent those most frequently overlooked by construction employers and standards covering situations that are particularly hazardous.

For the top 100 citations, the ranking is in **bold text** at the end of the regulation.

Note: In some references in this section, you will find a general industry regulation referenced along with the construction reference, i.e., (§1926.59/§1910.1200). This is because OSHA, in an effort to save printing costs for duplicating identical rules, has removed the text from the construction rules (Part 1926) and references you to the general industry rules (Part 1910) for the regulation.

General safety and health provisions—§1926.20

Contractor requirements

No contractor or subcontractor can require employees to work in surroundings or under working conditions which are unsanitary, hazardous, or dangerous to their health or safety. §1926.20(a)

Accident prevention responsibilities

- It is the employer's responsibility to initiate and maintain programs necessary to comply with the requirements of the construction regulations. §1926.20(b)(1)   **#17**

- The company's programs must provide for frequent and regular inspections of jobsites, materials, and equipment. Inspections must be made by a competent person designated by the employer. §1926.20(b)(2)   **#10**

- The use of any machinery, tools, materials, or equipment which is not in compliance with any applicable requirement of the construction regulations is prohibited. Out of compliance machines, tools, materials, and equipment must either be identified as unsafe by tagging or locking the controls to render them inoperable or must be physically removed from the jobsite. §1926.20(b)(3)

- Only employees qualified by training or experience can operate equipment and machinery. §1926.20(b)(4)

Safety training and education—§1926.21

Employer responsibility

- Employers must instruct employees in the recognition and avoidance of unsafe conditions at their jobsite, and of the regulations applicable to their work environment to control or eliminate hazards or exposure to injuries or illnesses. §1926.21(b)(2)   **#5**

- Employees required to handle or use poisons, caustics, and other harmful substances must be instructed in their safe handling and use, and be made aware of the potential hazards, personal hygiene, and personal protective measures required. §1926.21(b)(3)

- Employees required to handle or use flammable liquids, gases, or toxic materials must be instructed in the safe use and handling of these materials and made aware of regulations applicable to them. §1926.21(b)(5)

- Employees that enter confined spaces or enclosed spaces must be instructed as to the nature of the hazards involved, the necessary precautions to be taken, and in the use of protective and emergency equipment required. §1926.21(b)(6)

Housekeeping—§1926.25

- Form and scrap lumber with protruding nails, and all other debris must be kept clear from all work areas, passageways, and stairs, and in and around buildings or other structures. §1926.25(a)   **#28**

- Combustible scrap and debris, garbage, and other wastes must be safely removed at regular intervals. §1926.25(b), (c)

- Containers must be provided for collection and separation of all refuse. Covers must be provided on containers used for flammable or harmful substances. §1926.25(c)

Means of egress—§1926.34

General

No lock or fastening to prevent free escape from the inside of any building shall be installed. §1926.34(a)

Exit markings

Exits must be marked by readily visible signs. Access to exits must be marked by readily visible signs in all cases where the exit or way to reach it is not immediately visible. §1926.34(b)

Key Construction Regulation Summaries

Maintenance and workmanship

Means of escape must be continually maintained free of all obstructions to full instant use in the case of fire or other emergency. §1926.34(c)

Employee emergency action plans—§1926.35

When an emergency action plan is required by a particular OSHA standard, it must be in writing (except as provided in §1926.35(e)(3)), and must cover those designated actions employers and employees must take to ensure employee safety from fire and other emergencies. §1926.35

Medical services and first aid—§1926.50

- Before a project starts, plans must be made for prompt medical attention in case of serious injury. §1926.50(b)

- When a medical facility is not reasonably accessible (time and distance) for the treatment of injured employees, a person trained to render first aid must be available at the jobsite. §1926.50(c)   **#84**

- When needed, first aid supplies must be easily accessible. §1926.50(d)

- You must provide either proper equipment for prompt transportation of an injured person to a doctor or hospital, or a communication system to contact an ambulance service. §1926.50(e)

- In areas where 911 service is not available, the telephone numbers of physicians, hospitals, or ambulances must be conspicuously posted. §1926.50(f)

- Where any employee's eyes or body may be exposed to injurious corrosive materials, immediate emergency drenching or flushing facilities must be provided at the jobsite. §1926.50(g)

Sanitation—§1926.51

Potable water

- An adequate supply of potable water must be provided in all places of employment. §1926.51(a)(1)

- A common drinking cup is prohibited. §1926.51(a)(4)

Toilets at construction jobsites

Toilets must be provided at construction jobsites according to the following table. §1926.51(c)(1)

Number of employees	Minimum number of facilities
20 or less	1
20 or more	1 toilet seat and 1 urinal per 40 employees
200 or more	1 toilet seat and 1 urinal per 50 employees

Washing facilities

Adequate washing facilities must be provided when employees are applying paints, coatings, herbicides, or insecticides, or in other operations where contaminants may be harmful to employees. The facilities must be near the worksite and must be equipped to enable employees to remove the harmful substances. §1926.51(f)(1)

Occupational noise exposure—§1926.52

- When employees are subjected to sound levels exceeding those listed in the following table, feasible administrative or engineering controls must be implemented. §1926.52(b)

Permissible Noise Exposures

Duration per day, hours	Sound level dBA slow response
8	90
6	92
4	95
3	97
2	100
1½	102
1	105
½	110
¼ or less	115

- When engineering or administrative controls fail to reduce sound levels within the limits of the above table, personal protective equipment (29 CFR 1926, Subpart E) must be provided and used to reduce sound levels within the levels indicated. §1926.52(b)

- In all cases where sound levels exceed the values shown in the above Permissible Noise Exposures table, employers must implement and administer a continuing, effective, hearing conservation program. §1926.52(d)(1)

Key Construction Regulation Summaries

- Exposure to impulsive or impact noise should not exceed 140 dB peak sound pressure level. §1926.52(e)

Nonionizing radiation (lasers)—§1926.54

- Only qualified and trained employees shall be assigned to install, adjust, and operate laser equipment. §1926.54(a)

- Proof of qualification must be available and in the laser operator's possession at all times. §1926.54(b)

- Areas in which lasers are used must be posted with standard laser warning placards. §1926.54(d)

Gases, vapors, fumes, dusts, and mists—§1926.55

- Employees must avoid exposure by inhalation, ingestion, skin absorption, or contact with toxic gases, vapors, fumes, dusts, and mists at a concentration above those specified in the *Threshold Limit Values of Airborne Contaminants for 1970* of the ACGIH. §1926.55(a)

- Whenever feasible, administrative or engineering controls must first be implemented to comply with threshold limit values. §1926.55(b)

- When engineering and administrative controls are not feasible to achieve full compliance, protective equipment or other protective measures must be used to keep employee exposure to air contaminants within the limits prescribed. Any equipment and technical measures used for this purpose must first be approved for each particular use by a competent industrial hygienist or other technically qualified person. §1926.55(b)

Illumination—§1926.56

While work is in progress, construction areas, ramps, runways, corridors, offices, shops, and storage areas must be lighted to not less than the minimum illumination intensities listed in the table *Minimum Illumination Intensities in Foot-Candles* (see next page). §1926.56(a)

Minimum Illumination Intensities in Foot-Candles

Foot-candles	Area or operation
5	General construction area lighting.
3	General construction areas, concrete placement, excavation and waste areas, accessways, active storage areas, loading platforms, refueling, and field maintenance areas.
5	Indoors: warehouses, corridors, hallways, and exitways.
5	Tunnels, shafts, and general underground work areas: (Exception: minimum of 10 foot-candles is required at tunnel and shaft heading during drilling, mucking, and scaling. Bureau of Mines approved cap lights shall be acceptable for use in the tunnel heading.)
10	General construction plant and shops (e.g., batch plants, screening plants, mechanical and electrical equipment rooms, carpenters' shops, rigging lofts and active storerooms, barracks or living quarters, locker or dressing rooms, mess halls, indoor toilets, and workrooms).
30	First aid stations, infirmaries, and offices.

For areas or operations not covered above, consult American National Standard A11.1-1965, R1970, *Practice for Industrial Lighting* for recommended values of illumination.

Hazard communication—§1910.1200

Note: The construction regulations at 29 CFR 1926.59 (Hazard communication) refer you to 29 CFR 1910.1200 for hazard communication requirements.

Written hazard communication program

- Employers must develop, implement, and maintain at each worksite, a written hazard communication program. The program must at least describe how the requirements for labels and other forms of warning, material safety data sheets, and employee information and training will be met. §1910.1200(e)(1)   **#13**

- The program must also include:

    - A list of the hazardous chemicals known to be present at the jobsite. The list must use an identity that is referenced on the appropriate material safety data sheet. The list may be compiled for the worksite as a whole, or for individual work areas.

    - The methods employers will use to inform employees of the hazards of nonroutine tasks such as the cleaning of reactor vessels, and the hazards associated with chemicals contained in unlabeled pipes in their work areas.

Key Construction Regulation Summaries

- *Multi-employer worksites*—Employers who produce, use, or store hazardous chemicals at worksites in such a way that employees of other employer(s) may be exposed must additionally ensure that their hazard communication program includes the methods they will use to: (1) provide other employers on-site access to MSDSs for each hazardous chemical the other employer's employees may be exposed to, and (2) inform the other employers of any precautionary measures to be taken to protect their employees. §1910.1200(e)(2)

- Employers must make the written hazard communication program available, upon request, to employees, their designated representatives, and OSHA. §1910.1200(e)(4)

Labels and other forms of warning

Employers must ensure that each container of hazardous chemicals at a worksite is labeled, tagged, or marked with the identity of the hazardous chemical(s). Labels must also show hazard warnings appropriate for employee protection including specific information regarding the chemical's physical and health hazards. §1910.1200(f)(5)   **#81**

Material safety data sheets

- Employers must have a material safety data sheet at the worksite for each hazardous chemical their employees use. §1910.1200(g)(1)   **#39**

- Employers must ensure that employees have ready access to MSDSs during each work shift when they are at their worksites. Electronic access, microfiche, and other alternatives to maintaining paper copies of the MSDSs are permitted as long as no barriers to immediate employee access at each worksite are created by such options. §1910.1200(g)(8)   **#44**

Employee information and training

- Employers must provide employees with effective information and training on hazardous chemicals in their work area at the time of their initial assignment, and whenever a new physical or health hazard they have not previously been trained on is introduced. §1910.1200(h)   **#40**,   §1910.1200(h)(1)   **#38**

- Employers must provide employees with information on: (1) operations at their jobsite where hazardous chemicals are present, (2) the location and availability of the written hazard communication program including the required list(s) of hazardous chemicals, and the material safety data sheets, and (3) the requirements of the regulation. §1910.1200(h)(2)

- Employee training must include at least: (1) methods and observations (such as monitoring, odor, etc.) that may be used to detect the presence or release of a hazardous chemical, (2) the physical and health hazards of the chemicals at the worksite, (3) the measures employees can take to protect themselves from the hazards, and (4) the details of the hazard communication program. §1910.1200(h)(3)

Lead—§1926.62

Permissible exposure limit

Employers must ensure that no employee is exposed to lead at concentrations in excess of the permissible exposure limit (PEL). The PEL is an eight-hour time weighted average (TWA) of 50 micrograms per cubic meter of air (50 µg/m^3). §1926.62(c)(1)

Exposure assessment

- Employers who have a jobsite or operation covered by the lead standard must initially determine if any employee may be exposed to lead at or above the action level. Employee exposure is that exposure which would occur if the employee were not using a respirator. With the exceptions provided in the regulation at §1926.62(d)(3), personal samples must be gathered under the conditions in .62(d)(1)(iii). §1926.62(d)(1)   **#71**

- Until employers perform an employee exposure assessment as required in paragraph (d) of the lead standard, and documents that the employee performing any of the listed tasks is not exposed above the PEL, employers must treat the employee as if he/she were exposed above the PEL, and not in excess of 10 times the PEL, and must implement employee protective measures prescribed in the lead standard. §1926.62(d)(2) **#49**

Methods of compliance

- Employers must implement engineering, administrative, and work practice controls to the extent feasible to reduce and maintain employee exposure below the PEL. When these controls are not sufficient, they must still be implemented and then supplemented with respiratory protection. §1926.62(e)(1)

- Prior to starting a job, employers must establish and implement a written compliance program to achieve compliance with the requirements of the lead standard. §1926.62(e)(2)

Respiratory protection

- For employees who use respirators required by the lead standard, the respirators must comply with §1926.62(f)—Respiratory protection. §1926.62(f)(1)

- Employers must implement a respiratory protection program in accordance with the OSHA general industry requirements at 29 CFR 1910.134(b) through (d) (except (d)(1)(iii)), and (f) through (m). §1926.62(f)(2)

- Employers must select appropriate respirators or a combination of respirators from Table 1 of the lead standard. §1926.62(f)(3)

Key Construction Regulation Summaries

Protective work clothing and equipment/Hygiene facilities and practices

- Where employees are exposed to lead above the PEL (without respirators), and where employees are exposed to lead compounds that may cause skin or eye irritation, and when protecting employees during exposure assessment, employers must provide at no cost to employees and assure that the employees use appropriate protective work clothing and equipment that prevents contamination of the employees and their garments. §1926.62(g)(1)

- Employers must provide:

  - The required protective work clothing in a clean and dry condition at least weekly, and daily when exposure levels are, without regard to a respirator, over 200 µg/m^3 of lead as an 8-hour TWA. §1926.62(g)(2)

  - Clean change areas for employees whose airborne exposure to lead is above the PEL, and as interim protection for employees performing tasks as specified in §1926.62(d)(2) without regard to the used of respirators. §1926.62(i)(2)

  - Shower facilities, where feasible, for use by employees whose airborne exposure is above the PEL. §1926.62(i)(3)

  - Lunchroom facilities or eating areas for employees whose airborne exposure to lead is above the PEL, without regard to the use of respirators. §1926.62(i)(4)

  - Adequate hand washing facilities in accordance with 1926.51(f). §1926.62(i)(5)

Employee information and training

- Employers must communicate information to employees concerning lead hazards according to the requirements of OSHA's Hazard Communication Standard including but not limited to the requirements concerning warning signs and labels, material safety data sheets, and employee information and training. §1926.62(l)(1)

- Employers must assure that each employee involved in lead operations is trained in the requirements of §1926.62(l)(2).

Signs

Employers must post the following warning sign in each work area where employee exposure to lead is above the PEL:

WARNING
LEAD WORK AREA
POISON
NO SMOKING OR EATING

§1926.62(m)(2)

Personal protective equipment (PPE)—§1926, Subpart E

Criteria for PPE

- Employers must ensure their employees wear appropriate personal protective equipment (PPE): (1) in all operations where there is an exposure to hazardous conditions, or (2) where an OSHA regulation indicates there is a need for wearing PPE to reduce employee exposure to a hazardous situation. §1926.28(a)   **#58**

- Protective equipment—including personal protective equipment for eyes, face, head, and extremities—protective clothing, respiratory devices, and protective shields and barriers, must be provided, used, and maintained in a sanitary and reliable condition wherever it is necessary by reason of hazards of processes or environment, chemical hazards, radiological hazards, or mechanical irritants encountered in a manner capable of causing injury or impairment in the function of any part of an employee's body through absorption, inhalation, or physical contact. §1926.95(a)   **#36**

- Where employees furnish their own personal protective equipment, employers are responsible to assure its adequacy and that the equipment is properly maintained and in a sanitary condition. §1926.95(b)

Foot protection

Safety-toe footwear must meet the requirements of ANSI Z41.1-1967, *Standard for Men's Safety-Toe Footwear.* §1926.96

Head protection

Employees must be protected by protective helmets when they work in areas where there is a possible danger of head injury from impact, falling or flying objects, or electrical shocks and burns. §1926.100(a)   **#3**

Hearing protection

- When it is not feasible to reduce noise levels or duration of exposures to those specified in the Permissible Noise Exposures table (page 14), ear protective devices must be provided and used. §1926.101(a)

- Plain cotton is not an acceptable protective device. §1926.101(c)

Eye and face protection

- Employees must be provided with eye and face protection when machines or operations present potential eye or face injury from physical, chemical, or radiation agents. §1926.102(a)(1)   **#27**

- Eye and face protective equipment must meet the requirements of ANSI Z87.1-1968, *Practice for Occupational and Educational Eye and Face Protection.* §1926.102(a)(2)

Key Construction Regulation Summaries

Respiratory protection

Note: The construction regulations at 29 CFR 1926.103 (Respiratory protection) refer you to 29 CFR 1910.134 for respiratory protection requirements.

- In the control of occupational diseases caused by breathing air contaminated with harmful dusts, fogs, fumes, mists, gases, smokes, sprays, or vapors, the primary objective must be to prevent atmospheric contamination. This must be accomplished as far as feasible by accepted engineering control measures. When effective engineering controls are not feasible, or while they are being instituted, appropriate respirators must be used. §1910.134(a)(1)

- Respirators must be provided when they are necessary to protect the health of employees. Respirators provided must be applicable and suitable for the purpose intended. §1910.134(a)(2)

- Employers are responsible for the establishment and maintenance of a respiratory protection program meeting the requirements of §1910.134(c). §1910.134(a)(2)

- In any workplace where respirators are necessary to protect the health of employees or required by an employer, the employer must establish and implement a written respiratory protection program with worksite-specific procedures. The program must be updated as necessary to reflect changes in workplace conditions that affect respirator use. Employers must include in the program the provisions found in §1910.134(c)(1)(i)-(ix), as applicable. §1910.134(c)(1)   **#47**

- Employers must select and provide an appropriate respirator based on the respiratory hazard(s) to which the worker is exposed and workplace and user factors that affect respiratory performance and reliability. §1910.134(d)(1)(i)   **#64**

- Employers must provide a medical evaluation to determine an employee's ability to use a respirator, before the employee is fit tested or required to use the respirator in the workplace. Employers may discontinue an employee's medical evaluations when the employee is no longer required to use a respirator. §1910.134(e)(1)   **#62**

Safety nets

Safety nets must be provided when workplaces are more than 25 feet above the surface and where the use of ladders, scaffolds, catch platforms, temporary floors, safety lines, or safety belts is impractical. §1926.105(a)   **#50**

Working over or near water

- Employees working over or near water, where the danger of drowning exists, must be provided coast guard approved life jackets or boyant work vests. §1926.106(a)

- Ring buoys with at least 90 feet of line must be provided and readily available. The distance between ring buoys must not exceed 200 ft. §1926.106(c)

- 21 -

- At least one lifesaving skiff must be immediately available where employees are working over or near water. §1926.106(d)

Fire protection—§1926.150

General requirements

- A fire fighting program must be developed and followed throughout all phases of construction and/or demolition work. The program must provide for effective fire fighting equipment to be available without delay, and designed to effectively meet all possible fire hazards. §1926.150(a)(1)

- Fire fighting equipment must be: (1) conspicuously located and readily accessible at all times, (2) periodically inspected, and (3) maintained in an operating condition. §1926.150(a)(2), (3), (4)

Portable firefighting equipment

A fire extinguisher, rated not less than 2A, must be provided for each 3,000 square feet of the protected building area, or major fraction thereof. Travel distance to the nearest fire extinguisher must not exceed 100 feet. §1926.150(c)(1)   **#34**

Fire prevention—§1926.151

Ignition hazards

Smoking is prohibited at or in the vicinity of operations which are a fire hazard. The operation must be conspicuously posted: NO SMOKING OR OPEN FLAME. §1926.151(a)(3)

Open yard storage

In outdoor storage areas, portable fire extinguishing equipment suitable for the fire hazard involved, must be provided at convenient, conspicuously accessible locations. The extinguishers, rated at not less than 2A, must be placed so that maximum travel distance to the nearest unit cannot exceed 100 feet. §1926.151(c)(6)

Flammable and combustible liquids—§1926.152

General requirements

Only approved containers and portable tanks can be used for storage and handling of flammable and combustible liquids. Approved safety cans, or Department of Transportation

Key Construction Regulation Summaries

approved containers can be used for the handling and use of flammable liquids in quantities of five gallons or less. For quantities of one gallon or less, the original container may be used for storage, use, and handling. §1926.152(a)(1)   **#91**

Indoor storage of flammable and combustible liquids

- No more than 25 gallons of flammable or combustible liquids can be stored in a room outside of an approved storage cabinet. For LPG storage, see §1926.153 in the construction regulations. §1926.152(b)(1)

- No more than 60 gallons of flammable or 120 gallons of combustible liquids can be stored in any one storage cabinet. No more than three storage cabinets may be located in a single storage area. §1926.152(b)(3)

Dispensing liquids

- Flammable or combustible liquids must be drawn from or transferred into vessels, containers, or tanks within a building or outside only through a closed piping system, from safety cans, by means of a device drawing through the top, or from a container, or portable tanks, by gravity or pump, through an approved self-closing valve. Transferring by means of air pressure on the container or portable tanks is prohibited. §1926.152(e)(3)

- The dispensing units must be protected against collision damage. §1926.152(e)(4)

Handling liquids at point of final use

Flammable liquids must be kept in closed containers when not actually in use. §1926.152(f)(1)

Service and refueling areas

- Conspicuous and legible signs prohibiting smoking must be posted in service and refueling areas. §1926.152(g)(9)

- Each service or fueling area must be provided with at least one fire extinguisher having a rating of not less than 20-B:C located so that an extinguisher will be within 75 feet of each pump, dispenser, underground fill pipe opening, and lubrication or service area. §1926.152(g)(11)

Liquified petroleum gas—§1926.153

Approval of equipment and systems

Each system must have containers, valves, connectors, manifold valve assemblies, and regulators of an approved type and must meet DOT specifications. §1926.153(a)

Safety devices

Every container and vaporizer must be provided with one or more approved safety relief valves or devices. The valves or devices must meet the requirements of §1926.153(d).

Containers and regulating equipment installed outside of buildings or structures

Containers must be placed upright on firm foundations or otherwise firmly secured. The possible effect on the outlet piping of settling must be guarded against by a flexible connection or special fitting. §1926.153(g)

Storage of LPG containers

Storage of LPG within buildings is prohibited. §1926.153(j)

Fire protection

Storage locations must have at least one approved portable fire extinguisher, rated not less than 20-B:C. §1926.153(l)

Temporary heating devices—§1926.154

Ventilation

- Fresh air must be supplied in sufficient quantities to maintain the health and safety of workers. Where natural means of fresh air is inadequate, mechanical ventilation must be provided. §1926.154(a)

- When heaters are used in confined spaces, special care must be taken to provide sufficient ventilation to: (1) ensure proper combustion, (2) maintain the health and safety of workers, and (3) limit temperature rise in the area. §1926.154(a)

Solid fuel salamanders

Solid fuel salamanders are prohibited in buildings and on scaffolds. §1926.154(d)

Oil-fired heaters

Flammable liquid-fired heaters must be equipped with a primary safety control to stop the flow of fuel in the event of flame failure. §1926.154(e)

Accident prevention signs and tags—§1926.200

General

Required signs and symbols must be visible at all times when work is being done, and promptly removed or covered when the hazard(s) no longer exist. §1926.200(a)

Key Construction Regulation Summaries

Caution signs

Caution signs must be used only to warn against potential hazards or caution against unsafe practices. §1926.200(c)

Traffic signs

Construction areas must be posted with legible traffic signs at the point of a hazard. §1926.200(g)(1)

Signaling—§1926.201

Flagmen

- When signs, signals, and barricades do not provide necessary protection on or adjacent to a highway or street, flagmen or other appropriate traffic controls must be provided. §1926.201(a)(1)

- Flagmen must be provided with and must wear a red or orange warning garment while flagging. Warning garments worn at night must be of reflectorized material. §1926.201(a)(4)

Materials storage—§1926.250

General

- All materials stored in tiers must be secured to prevent sliding, falling, or collapse. §1926.250(a)(1)

- Aisles and passageways must be kept clear and in good repair to provide for the free and safe movement of material handling equipment or employees. §1926.250(a)(3)

Material storage

- Material stored inside buildings under construction must not be placed within six feet of any hoistway or inside floor opening, nor within ten feet of an exterior wall which does not extend above the top of the material stored. §1926.250(b)(1)

- Used lumber must have all nails removed before stacking. §1926.250(b)(8)

Rigging equipment for materials handling—§1926.251

General

- Rigging equipment for material handling must be inspected prior to use on each shift and as necessary during use to ensure it is safe. Defective equipment must be removed from service. §1926.251(a)(1)

- Special custom designed grabs, hooks, clamps, or other lifting accessories—for such units as modular panels, prefabricated structures, and similar materials—must be marked to indicate the safe working loads, and must be proof-tested to 125 percent of their rated load prior to use. §1926.251(a)(4)

- Each day, before being used, the slings and all fastenings and attachments of rigging equipment must be inspected for damage or defects by an employer designated competent person. Additional inspections must be performed during sling use, where service conditions warrant. §1926.251(a)(6)

- Damaged or defective slings must be immediately removed from service. §1926.251(a)(6)

Alloy steel chains

- Welded alloy steel chains must have permanently affixed durable identification stating size, grade, rated capacity, and sling manufacturer. §1926.251(b)(1)

- In addition to the inspection required by other sections of §1926.251, a thorough periodic inspection of all alloy steel chain slings in use must be made. The frequency of the inspection must be determined by: frequency of sling use, severity of service conditions, nature of lifts being made, and experience gained on the service life of slings used in similar circumstances. The periodic inspection must never exceed one year. §1926.251(b)(6)

Wire rope

- The following limitations apply to the use of wire rope: §1926.251(c)(4)

    - An eye splice made in any wire rope must have at least three full tucks. However, this requirement shall not operate to preclude the use of another form of splice or connection which can be shown to be as efficient and which is not otherwise prohibited.

    - Except for eye splices in the ends of wires and for endless rope slings, each wire rope used in hoisting, lowering, or pulling loads, must be of one continuous piece without knot or splice.

    - Eyes in wire rope bridles, slings, or bull wires cannot be formed by wire rope clips or knots.

    - Wire rope must not be used if, in any length of eight diameters, the total number of visible broken wires exceeds 10 percent of the total number of wires, or if the rope shows other signs of excessive wear, corrosion, or defect.

Key Construction Regulation Summaries

- When U-bolt wire rope clips are used to form eyes, the following table must be used to determine the number and spacing of clips. §1926.251(c)(5)

Number and Spacing of U-Bolt Wire Rope Clips

Improved Plow Steel, Rope Diameter (inches)	Number of Clips — Drop Forged	Number of Clips — Other Material	Minimum Spacing (inches)
1/2	3	4	3
5/8	3	4	3 3/4
3/4	4	5	4 1/2
7/8	4	5	5 1/4
1	5	6	6
1 1/8	6	6	6 3/4
1 1/4	6	7	7 1/2
1 3/8	7	7	8 1/4
1 1/2	7	8	9

- When U-bolts are used for eye splices, the U-bolt must be applied so that the "U" section is in contact with the dead end of the rope. §1926.251(c)(5)(i)

Synthetic webbing (nylon, polyester, and polypropylene)

- Synthetic web slings must be immediately removed from service if any of the following conditions are present: §1926.251(e)(8)
    - Acid or caustic burns.
    - Melting or charring of any part of the sling surface.
    - Snags, punctures, tears, or cuts.
    - Broken or worn stitches.
    - Distorted fittings.

Waste material disposal—§1926.252

- Whenever materials are dropped more than 20 feet to any exterior point of a building, an enclosed chute must be used. §1926.252(a)

- When debris is dropped through holes in the floor without the use of chutes, the area where the material is dropped must be enclosed with barricades not less than six feet back from the projected edges of the opening above. Warning signs must be posted at each level. §1926.252(b)

- All scrap lumber, waste material, and rubbish must be removed from the immediate work area as work progresses. §1926.252(c)

- All solvent waste, oily rags, and flammable liquids must be kept in fire resistant covered containers until removed from the worksite. §1926.252(e)

Tools, hand and power—§1926, Subpart I

General requirements—Condition of tools

All hand and power tools and similar equipment, whether furnished by the employer or the employee, must be maintained in a safe condition. §1926.300(a)

General requirements—Guarding

- When power operated tools are designed to accommodate guards, they must be equipped with the guards when in use. §1926.300(b)(1)   **#90**

- Belts, gears, shafts, pulleys, sprockets, spindles, drums, fly wheels, chains, or other reciprocating, rotating, or moving parts of equipment must be guarded if the parts are exposed to contact by employees or otherwise create a hazard. §1926.300(b)(2)   **#96**

- The point-of-operation of machines must be guarded when the operation exposes an employee to injury. The point-of-operation guarding device must be designed to prevent operators from having any part of their body in the danger zone during the operating cycle. §1926.300(b)(4)

- Special hand tools for placing and removing material must permit easy handling of the material without the operator placing a hand in the danger zone. The tools may not be used in place of guarding, but only to supplement the protection provided. §1926.300(b)(4)

- When the periphery of the blades of a fan is less than 7 feet above the floor or working level, the blades must be guarded. The guard must have openings no larger than $1/2$-inch. §1926.300(b)(5)

General requirements—Personal protective equipment

Employees using hand and power tools and exposed to hazards of falling, flying, abrasive, and splashing objects, or exposed to harmful dusts, fumes, mists, vapors, or gases must be provided with the particular personal protective equipment necessary to protect them from the hazards. §1926.300(c)

Hand tools

- Employers must not issue or permit the use of unsafe hand tools. §1926.301(a)

Key Construction Regulation Summaries

- The wooden handles of tools must be kept free of splinters or cracks and be kept tight in the tool. §1926.301(d)

Power-operated hand tools—Electric power-operated tools

Electric power operated tools must either be an approved double-insulated type, or be properly grounded in accordance with the OSHA electrical regulations. §1926.302(a)(1)

Power-operated hand tools—Pneumatic power tools

- Pneumatic power tools must be positively secured to the hose or whip to prevent accidental disconnection. §1926.302(b)(1)

- Safety clips or retainers must be securely installed and maintained on pneumatic impact tools to prevent attachments from being accidentally disconnected. §1926.302(b)(2)

- All hoses exceeding $1/2$-inch inside diameter must have a safety device at the source of the supply or branch line to reduce pressure in case of hose failure. §1926.302(b)(7)

- Compressed air used for cleaning purposes must not exceed 30 psi and must be used with effective chip guarding and personal protective equipment. This requirement does not apply to concrete form, mill scale, and similar cleaning operations. §1926.302(b)(4)

Abrasive wheels and tools—Use of abrasive wheels

Cup type wheels used for external grinding must be protected by either a revolving cup guard or a band type guard. All other portable abrasive wheels used for external grinding must be provided with safety guards (protection hoods). §1926.303(c)(3)

Woodworking tools—Guarding

- Portable, power-driven, circular saws must be equipped with guards above and below the base plate or shoe. The upper guard must cover the saw to the depth of the teeth, except for the minimum arc required to permit the base to be tilted for bevel cuts. The lower guard must cover the saw to the depth of the teeth, except for the minimum arc required to allow proper retraction and contact with the work, and must automatically return to the covering position when the blade is removed from the work. §1926.304(d)

Woodworking tools—Other requirements

All woodworking tools and machinery must meet other applicable requirements of ANSI, 01.1-1961, *Safety Code for Woodworking Machinery.* §1926.304(f)   **#51**

Woodworking tools—Hand-fed crosscut table saws

Each circular crosscut table saw must be guarded by a hood meeting all the requirements of §1926.304(i)(1) (next bullet). §1926.304(h)(1)

- 29 -

Woodworking tools—Hand-fed ripsaws

Each circular hand-fed ripsaw must be guarded by a hood which completely encloses the portion of the saw above the table and that portion of the saw above the material being cut. The hood and mounting must be arranged so that the hood will automatically adjust itself to the thickness of and remain in contact with the material being cut but cannot offer any considerable resistance to insertion of material to saw or passage of the material being sawed. The hood must be made of adequate strength to resist blows and strains incidental to reasonable operation, adjusting, and handling, and must be so designed as to protect the operator from flying splinters and broken saw teeth. It must be made of material that is soft enough so that it will be unlikely to cause tooth breakage. The hood must be so mounted as to insure that its operation will be positive, reliable, and in true alignment with the saw; and the mounting must be adequate in strength to resist any reasonable side thrust or other force tending to throw it out of line. §1926.304(i)(1)

Mechanical power-transmission apparatus—Pulleys

Pulleys, any parts of which are seven feet or less from the floor or working platform, must be guarded in accordance with the requirements of §1926.307(m) and (o). Pulleys serving as balance wheels (e.g., punch presses), on which the point of contact between belt and pulley is more than 6 feet, 6 inches from the floor or platform may be guarded with a disk covering the spokes. §1926.307(d)(1)

Mechanical power-transmission apparatus—Belt, rope, and chain drives

Vertical and inclined belts must be enclosed by a guard conforming to §1926.307(m) and (o). All guards for inclined belts must be arranged so a minimum clearance of seven feet is maintained between belt and floor at any point outside of the guard. §1926.307(e)(3)

Welding and cutting—§1926, Subpart J

Gas welding and cutting—Transporting, moving, and storing compressed gas cylinders

- Valve protection caps must be installed when compressed gas cylinders are transported, moved, or stored. §1926.350(a)(1)

- A suitable cylinder truck, chain, or other steadying device must be used to keep cylinders from being knocked over while in use. §1926.350(a)(7)

- Compressed gas cylinders must be secured in an upright position at all times, except, if necessary, for short periods of time when cylinders are actually being hoisted or carried. §1926.350(a)(9)   **#53**

- Oxygen cylinders in storage must be separated from fuel-gas cylinders and combustible materials (especially oil or grease) a minimum distance of 20 feet, or by a noncombustible barrier at least five feet high having at least a $1/2$-hour fire-resistance rating. §1926.350(a)(10)   **#59**

Key Construction Regulation Summaries

- Inside of buildings, cylinders must be stored in a well-protected, well-ventilated, dry location at least 20 feet from highly combustible materials such as oil or excelsior. Cylinders should be stored in definitely assigned places away from elevators, stairs, or gangways. Assigned storage places must be located where cylinders will not be knocked over or damaged by passing or falling objects, or subject to tampering by unauthorized persons. Cylinders must not be kept in unventilated enclosures such as lockers and cupboards. §1926.350(a)(11)

Gas welding and cutting—Regulators and gauges

Oxygen and fuel gas regulators must be in proper working order while in use. §1926.350(h)

Gas welding and cutting—Additional rules

For additional details not covered in the construction gas welding and cutting regulations, applicable technical portions of the American National Standards Institute standard Z49.1-1967, *Safety in Welding and Cutting*, will apply. §1926.350(j)

Arc welding and cutting—Welding cables and connectors

- Only cable free from repair or splices for a minimum distance of 10 feet from the cable end to which the electrode holder is connected can be used—except that cables with standard insulated connectors or with splices whose insulating quality is equal to that of the cable are permitted. §1926.351(b)(2)

- Cables in need of repair must not be used. When a cable, other than the cable lead referred to in paragraph §1926.351(b)(2) [above] becomes worn to the extent of exposing bare conductors, the portion thus exposed must be protected by means of rubber and friction tape or other equivalent insulation. §1926.351(b)(4)

Arc welding and cutting—Shielding

Whenever practicable, all arc welding and cutting operations must be shielded by noncombustible or flame proof screens to protect employees from direct arc rays. §1926.351(e)

Fire prevention

Suitable fire extinguishing equipment must be immediately available in the work area and must be maintained in a state of readiness for instant use. §1926.352(d)

Ventilation and protection in welding, cutting, and heating

Employees performing any type of welding, cutting, or heating must be protected by suitable eye protection that meets the requirements of §1926, Subpart E. §1926.353(e)(2)

Electrical—§1926, Subpart K

General requirements—Approved equipment

- All electrical conductors and equipment must be approved. §1926.403(a)

- Employers must ensure that electrical equipment is free from recognized hazards that are likely to cause death or serious physical harm to employees. Safety of equipment will be determined by the requirements at §1926.403(b)(1)(i) through (vii). §1926.403(b)(1)   **#63**

General requirements—Examination, installation, and use of equipment

Listed, labeled, or certified equipment must be installed and used in accordance with instructions included in the listing, labeling, or certification. §1926.403(b)(2)   **#42**

General requirements—Mounting and cooling of equipment

Electric equipment must be firmly secured to its mounting surface. Wooden plugs driven into holes in masonry, concrete, plaster, or similar materials must not be used. §1926.403(d)(1)

General requirements—Splices

Conductors must be spliced or joined with splicing devices designed for the use or by brazing, welding, or soldering with a fusible metal or alloy. Soldered splices must first be so spliced or joined as to be mechanically and electrically secure without solder and then soldered. All splices and joints and the free ends of conductors must be covered with an insulation equivalent to that of the conductors or with an insulating device designed for the purpose. §1926.403(e).

General requirements—Marking

Electrical equipment must not be used unless the manufacturer's name, trademark, or other descriptive marking is on the equipment and unless other markings are provided giving voltage, current, wattage, or other ratings as necessary. The marking must be of sufficient durability to withstand the environment involved. §1926.403(g)

General requirements—Identification of disconnecting means and circuits

Each disconnecting means required by this subpart (§1926, Subpart K—Electrical) for motors and appliances must be legibly marked to indicate its purpose, unless located and arranged so the purpose is evident. Each service, feeder, and branch circuit, at its disconnecting means or over current device, must be legibly marked to indicate its purpose, unless located and arranged so the purpose is evident. These markings must be of sufficient durability to withstand the environment involved. §1926.403(h)   **#77**

Key Construction Regulation Summaries

General requirements—600 volts, nominal or less

- Sufficient access and working space must be provided and maintained about all electric equipment to permit ready and safe operation and maintenance of the equipment. The requirements for working clearances, clear space, access and entrance to working space, front working space, and headroom in §1926.403(i)(1)(i) through (v) apply. §1926.403(i)(1)

- Except as required or permitted elsewhere in this subpart (§1926, Subpart K—Electrical), live parts of electric equipment operating at 50 volts or more must be guarded against accidental contact by cabinets or other forms of enclosures, or by any of the means in §1926.403(i)(2)(i)(A) through (D). §1926.403(i)(2)   **#43**

Wiring design and protection—Use and identification of grounded and grounding conductors

No grounded conductor can be attached to any terminal or lead so as to reverse designated polarity. §1926.404(a)(2)

Wiring design and protection—Branch circuits—Ground fault protection

Employers must use either ground fault circuit interrupters or an assured equipment grounding conductor program to protect employees on construction sites. These requirements are in addition to any other requirements for equipment grounding conductors. Ground-fault circuit interrupter requirements are in §1926.404(b)(1)(ii) and the requirements for an assured equipment grounding conductor program are in §1926.404(b)(1)(iii). §1926.404(b)(1)   **#8**

Wiring design and protection—Grounding

- The path to ground from circuits, equipment, and enclosures must be permanent and continuous. §1926.404(f)(6)   **#26**

- Grounding requirements for supports, enclosures, and equipment must meet the requirements in §1926.404(f)(7). This includes supports and enclosures for conductors, fixed equipment, equipment connected by cord and plug, and nonelectrical equipment. §1926.404(f)(7)

Wiring methods, components, and equipment—Temporary wiring

The requirements for temporary electrical power and lighting wiring methods are found in §1926.405(a)(2). Temporary wiring may be of a class less than would be required for a permanent installation. Temporary wiring must be removed immediately upon completion of construction or the purpose for which the wiring was installed. Temporary wiring requirements include requirements for extension cords. §1926.405(a)(2)   **#22**

Wiring methods, components, and equipment—Cabinets, boxes and fittings

- Conductors entering boxes, cabinets, or fittings must be protected from abrasion, and openings through which conductors enter must be effectively closed. Unused openings in cabinets, boxes, and fittings must also be effectively closed. §1926.405(b)(1)   **#69**

- All pull boxes, junction boxes, and fittings must be provided with covers. If metal covers are used, they must be grounded. In energized installations, each outlet box must have a cover, faceplate, or fixture canopy. Covers of outlet boxes having holes through which flexible cord pendants pass must be provided with bushings designed for the purpose or shall have smooth, well-rounded surfaces on which the cords may bear. §1926.405(b)(2) **#52**

Wiring methods, components, and equipment—Switchboards and panelboards

Switchboards that have any exposed live parts must be located in permanently dry locations and accessible only to qualified persons. Panelboards must be mounted in cabinets, cutout boxes, or enclosures designed for the purpose and must be dead front. However, panelboards other than the dead front externally-operable type are permitted where accessible only to qualified persons. Exposed blades of knife switches must be dead when open. §1926.405(d)

Wiring methods, components, and equipment—Enclosures for damp or wet locations

Cabinets, cutout boxes, fittings, boxes, and panelboard enclosures in damp or wet locations must be installed to prevent moisture or water from entering and accumulating within the enclosures. In wet locations the enclosures must be weatherproof. §1926.405(e)(1)

Wiring methods, components, and equipment—Flexible cords and cables

- Flexible cords and cables must be suitable for conditions of use and location. Flexible cords and cables can be used only for those applications listed in §1926.405(g)(1)(i). Flexible cords and cables must not be used for the situations outlined in §1926.405(g)(1)(iii). §1926.405(g)(1)   **#85**

- Flexible cords and cables must be identified, spliced, and terminated in accordance with the following requirements: §1926.405(g)(2)   **#31**

    - A conductor of a flexible cord or cable that is used as a grounded conductor or an equipment grounding conductor must be distinguishable from other conductors.

    - Type SJ, SJO, SJT, SJTO, S, SO, ST, and STO cords must not be used unless durably marked on the surface with the type designation, size, and number of conductors.

    - Flexible cords must be used only in continuous lengths without splice or tap. Hard service flexible cords No. 12 or larger may be repaired if spliced so that the splice retains the insulation, outer sheath properties, and usage characteristics of the cord being spliced.

Key Construction Regulation Summaries

- Flexible cords must be connected to devices and fittings so that strain relief is provided which will prevent pull from being directly transmitted to joints or terminal screws.

- Flexible cords and cables must be protected by bushings or fittings where passing through holes in covers, outlet boxes, or similar enclosures.

Wiring methods, components, and equipment—Equipment for general use

- Lighting fixtures, lamp holders, lamps, and receptacles must meet the OSHA requirements found in §1926.405(j)(1).   **#87**

- Receptacles, cord connectors, and attachment plugs (caps) must meet the requirements of §1926.405(j)(2).

Safety related work practices—Protection of employees

- Employers must not permit an employee to work close to any part of an electric power circuit that the employee could contact while working, unless the employee is protected against electric shock by deenergizing the circuit and grounding it or by guarding it effectively by insulation or other means. §1926.416(a)(1)   **#74**

- Before work is started, employers must make sure—by inquiry, direct observation, or instruments—whether any part of an energized electric power circuit, exposed or concealed, is so located that the performance of the work may bring any person, tool, or machine into physical or electrical contact with the electric power circuit. Employers must post and maintain proper warning signs where such a circuit exists. Employers must advise employees of the location of such lines, the hazards involved, and the protective measures to be taken. §1926.416(a)(3)

Safety related work practices—Passageways and open spaces

Working spaces, walkways, and similar locations must be kept clear of cords so as not to create a hazard to employees. §1926.416(b)(2)

Safety related work practices—Cords and cables

Worn or frayed electric cords or cables must not be used. §1926.416(e)(1)   **#55**

Lockout and tagging of circuits

- Controls to be deactivated during the course of work on energized or deenergized equipment of circuits must be tagged. §1926.417(a)

- Equipment or circuits that are deenergized must be rendered inoperative and must be locked out or tagged out at all points where the equipment or circuits could be energized. §1926.417(b)

- Tags must be placed to identify plainly the equipment or circuits being worked on. §1926.417(c)

Scaffolding—§1926, Subpart L

Subpart L of the OSHA regulations applies to all scaffolds used in workplaces covered by the 29 CFR 1926 construction regulations. It does not apply to crane or derrick suspended personnel platforms, which are covered by §1926.550(g). This regulation does cover aerial lifts.

General requirements—Capacity

- Except as provided in §1926.451(a)(2) through (a)(5) and (g), each scaffold and scaffold component must be capable of supporting, without failure, its own weight and at least four times the maximum intended load applied or transmitted to it. §1926.451(a)(1)

- Scaffolds must be designed by a qualified person and must be constructed and loaded in accordance with that design. §1926.451(a)(6)

General requirements—Scaffold platform construction

- Each platform on all working levels of scaffolds must be fully planked or decked between the front uprights and the guardrail supports according to the requirements at §1926.451(b)(1)(i) and (ii).   **#7**

- Except as provided in §1926.451(b)(2)(i) and (ii), each scaffold platform and walkway must be at least 18 inches wide. §1926.451(b)(2)   **#70**

- Each end of a platform, unless cleated or otherwise restrained by hooks or equivalent means, must extend over the centerline of its support at least six inches. §1926.451(b)(4)

- Each end of a platform 10 feet or less in length must not extend over its support more than 12 inches unless the platform is designed and installed so that the cantilevered portion of the platform is able to support employees and/or materials without tipping, or has guardrails which block employee access to the cantilevered end. Each platform greater than 10 feet in length must not extend over its support more than 18 inches, unless it is designed and installed so that the cantilevered portion of the platform is able to support employees without tipping, or has guardrails which block employee access to the cantilevered end. §1926.451(b)(5)   **#73**

General requirements—Criteria for supported scaffolds

- Supported scaffolds with a height to base width (including outrigger supports, if used) ratio of more than four to one (4:1) must be restrained from tipping by guying, tying, bracing, or equivalent means, according to the requirements of §1926.451(c)(1).   **#60**

- Supported scaffold poles, legs, posts, frames, and uprights must bear on base plates and mud sills or other adequate firm foundation and must follow the requirements of §1926.451(c)(2).   **#9**

- Supported scaffold poles, legs, posts, frames, and uprights must be plumb and braced to prevent swaying and displacement. §1926.451(c)(3)   **#88**

Key Construction Regulation Summaries

General requirements—Access

- When scaffold platforms are more than two feet above or below a point of access, portable, hook-on, and attachable ladders; stair towers (scaffold stairways/towers); stairway-type ladders (such as ladder stands); ramps; walkways; integral prefabricated scaffold access; or direct access from another scaffold, structure, personnel hoist, or similar surface; must be used. Crossbraces must not be used as a means of access. §1926.451(e)(1) **#6**

- Ramps and walkways six feet or more above lower levels must have guardrail systems installed complying with Subpart M—Fall protection of the OSHA construction regulations. §1926.451(e)(5)

- Integral prefabricated scaffold access frames must meet the requirements of §1926.451(e)(6)(i) through (vi).

- Access for employees erecting or dismantling supported scaffolds must be in accordance with the requirements of §1926.451(e)(9)(i) through (iv).

General requirements—Use

- Scaffolds and scaffold components must not be loaded in excess of their maximum intended loads or rated capacities, whichever is less. §1926.451(f)(1)

- Scaffolds and scaffold components must be inspected for visible defects by a competent person before each work shift, and after any occurrence which could affect the scaffold's structural integrity. §1926.451(f)(3) **#32**

- Any part of a scaffold damaged or weakened such that its strength is less than that required by §1926.451(a) must be immediately repaired or replaced, braced to meet those provisions, or removed from service until repaired. §1926.451(f)(4) **#76**

- The clearance between scaffolds and power lines must be per the chart at §1926.451(f)(6). Scaffolds must not be erected, used, dismantled, altered, or moved so that they or any conductive material handled on them might come closer to exposed and energized power lines than the distances in the chart. §1926.451(f)(6)

- Scaffolds must be erected, moved, dismantled, or altered only under the supervision and direction of a competent person qualified in scaffold erection, moving, dismantling or alteration. The activities must be performed only by experienced and trained employees selected for the work by the competent person. §1926.451(f)(7) **#25**

- Debris must not be allowed to accumulate on platforms. §1926.451(f)(13)

- Ladders must not be used on scaffolds to increase the working level height of employees, except on large area scaffolds where employers have satisfied the criteria in §1926.451(f)(15).

General requirements—Fall protection

- Each employee on a scaffold more than 10 feet above a lower level must be protected from falling to that lower level. Section 1926.451(g)(1) (i) through (vii) establishes the types of fall protection to be provided to employees on each type of scaffold. Section 1926.451(g)(2) addresses fall protection for scaffold erectors and dismantlers. §1926.451(g)(1)   **#1**

- Employers must have a competent person determine the feasibility and safety of providing fall protection for employees erecting or dismantling supported scaffolds. Employers are required to provide fall protection for employees erecting or dismantling supported scaffolds where the installation and use of such protection is feasible and does not create a greater hazard. §1926.451(g)(2)

- In addition to meeting the requirements of §1926.502(d), personal fall arrest systems used on scaffolds must be attached by lanyard to a vertical lifeline, horizontal lifeline, or scaffold structural member. Vertical lifelines must not be used when overhead components, such as overhead protection or additional platform levels, are part of a single-point or two-point adjustable suspension scaffold. See §1926.451(g)(3)(i) through (iv) for lifeline requirements. §1926.451(g)(3)

- Guardrail systems installed to meet the requirements of the scaffold regulations must comply with the provisions in §1926.451(g)(4)(i) through (xv). Guardrail systems built in accordance with §1926 Subpart L, Appendix A, will be deemed to meet the requirements of paragraphs (g)(4) (vii), (viii), and (ix) of §1926.451(g)(4).   **#23**

General requirements—Falling object protection

- In addition to wearing hard hats, employees on a scaffold must be provided with additional protection from falling hand tools, debris, and other small objects by installing toeboards, screens, or guardrail systems, or through the erection of debris nets, catch platforms, or canopy structures that contain or deflect the falling objects. When the falling objects are too large or heavy to be contained or deflected by any of the above-listed measures, employers must place such potential falling objects away from the edge of the surface from which they could fall and must secure those materials as necessary to prevent their falling. §1926.451(h)(1)   **#78**

- Where there is a danger of tools, materials, or equipment falling from a scaffold and striking employees below, the provisions in §1926.451(h)(2)(i) through (v) will apply. **#61**

Requirements for specific scaffolds—Fabricated frame scaffolds (tubular welded frame scaffolds)

- Frames and panels must be braced by cross, horizontal, or diagonal braces, or combination thereof, which secure vertical members together laterally. The cross braces must be of a length that will automatically square and align vertical members so that the erected scaffold is always plumb, level, and square. All brace connections must be secured. §1926.452(c)(2)   **#37**

Key Construction Regulation Summaries

- Frames and panels must be joined together vertically by coupling or stacking pins or equivalent means. §1926.452(c)(3)

- Where uplift can occur which could displace scaffold end frames or panels, the frames or panels must be locked together vertically by pins or equivalent means. §1926.452(c)(4) **#98**

Requirements for specific scaffolds—Pump jack scaffolds

- Poles must be secured to the structure by rigid triangular bracing or equivalent at the bottom, top, and other points as necessary. When the pump jack has to pass bracing already installed, an additional brace must be installed approximately four feet above the brace to be passed, and must be left in place until the pump jack has been moved and the original brace reinstalled. §1926.452(j)(2)

- When poles are made of wood, the pole lumber must be straight-grained, free of shakes, large loose or dead knots, and other defects which might impair strength. §1926.452(j)(5) **#93**

- When two by fours are spliced to make a pole, mending plates must be installed at all splices to develop the full strength of the member. §1926.452(j)(7)

Requirements for specific scaffolds—Ladder jack scaffolds

Platforms must not exceed 20 feet in height. §1926.452(k)(1)

Requirements for specific scaffolds—Mobile scaffolds

- Scaffolds must be braced by cross, horizontal, or diagonal braces, or combination thereof, to prevent racking or collapse of the scaffold and to secure vertical members together laterally so as to automatically square and align the vertical members. Scaffolds must be plumb, level, and squared. All brace connections must be secured. Scaffolds constructed of tube and coupler components must also comply with the requirements of §1926.452(b). Scaffolds constructed of fabricated frame components must also comply with the requirements of paragraph §1926.452(c). §1926.452(w)(1)

- Scaffold casters and wheels must be locked with positive wheel and/or wheel and swivel locks, or equivalent means, to prevent movement of the scaffold while it is stationary. §1926.452(w)(2)

- Employees must not be allowed to ride on scaffolds unless the conditions in §1926.452(w)(6)(i) through (v) are met.

Aerial lifts—General requirements

- Unless otherwise provided in §1926.453, aerial lifts acquired for use on or after January 22, 1973 must be designed and constructed in conformance with the applicable requirements of the American National Standards for *Vehicle Mounted Elevating and Rotating Work Platforms*, ANSI A92.2-1969. Aerial lifts acquired before January 22, 1973, which do not meet the requirements of ANSI A92.2-1969, may not be used after January 1, 1976, unless they are modified so they conform with the applicable design and construction requirements of ANSI A92.2-1969. §1926.453(a)(1)

- Aerial lifts may be "field modified" for uses other than those intended by the manufacturer provided the modification has been certified in writing by the manufacturer or by any other equivalent entity, such as a nationally recognized testing laboratory, to be in conformity with all applicable provisions of ANSI A92.2-1969 and §1926.453 and to be at least as safe as the equipment was before modification. §1926.453(a)(2)

Aerial lifts—Extensible and articulating boom platforms

Lift controls must be tested each day prior to use to determine that they are in safe working condition. Extensible and articulating boom platform operators and equipment must also meet the requirements of §1926.453(b)(2)(i) through (xii). **#14**

Scaffold training requirements

- Employees who work on scaffolds must be trained—by a person qualified in the subject matter—to recognize hazards associated with the type of scaffold being used and to understand the procedures to control or minimize those hazards. The training must include the requirements in §1926.454(a)(1) through (a)(5). **#16**

- Employees who erect, disassemble, move, operate, repair, maintain, or inspect scaffolds must be trained by a competent person to recognize any hazards associated with the work in question. The training must include the requirements of §1926.454(b)(1) through (b)(4). **#54**

- When employers have reason to believe that an employee lacks the skill or understanding needed for safe work involving the erection, use, or dismantling of scaffolds, the employer must retrain that employee so that the requisite proficiency is regained. Retraining is required in at least the situations stated in §1926.454(c)(1) through (c)(3).

Fall protection—§1926, Subpart M

Subpart M of the OSHA regulations sets forth requirements and criteria for fall protection in construction workplaces covered under 29 CFR part §1926. Exception: The provisions of this subpart do not apply when employees are making an inspection, investigation, or assessment of workplace conditions prior to the actual start of construction work or after all construction work has been completed.

Fall protection requirements for the following work areas are not provided in Subpart M but are found in the following respective Subparts of the OSHA construction regulations:

- Working on scaffolds—Subpart L.

- Working on certain cranes and derricks—Subpart N.

Key Construction Regulation Summaries

- Performing steel erection work—§1926.105 and Subpart R.

- Working on certain types of equipment used in tunneling operations—Subpart S.

- Engaged in the construction of electric transmission/distribution lines and equipment—Subpart V.

- Working on stairways and ladders—Subpart X.

Duty to have fall protection

- ***General***—Employers must determine if the walking/working surfaces on which their employees will work have the strength and structural integrity to support employees safely. Employees can work on those surfaces only when the surfaces have the required strength and structural integrity. §1926.501(a)(2)

- ***Unprotected sides and edges***—Each employee on a walking/working surface (horizontal or vertical) with an unprotected side or edge six feet or more above a lower level must be protected from falling by the use of a guardrail, safety net, or personal fall arrest system. §1926.501(b)(1) **#2**

- ***Leading edges***—Employees constructing leading edges six feet or more above lower levels must be protected from falling by guardrail, safety net, or personal fall arrest systems. §1926.501(b)(2) **#82**

- ***Hoist areas***—Employees in a hoist area must be protected from falling 6 feet or more to lower levels by guardrail systems or personal fall arrest systems. If guardrail systems, [or chain, gate, or guardrail] or portions thereof, are removed to facilitate the hoisting operation (e.g., during landing of materials), and an employee must lean through the access opening or out over the edge of the access opening (to receive or guide equipment and materials, for example), that employee shall be protected from fall hazards by a personal fall arrest system. §1926.501(b)(3) **#86**

- ***Holes***—Employees on walking/working surfaces must be protected from: (1) falling through holes (including skylights) more than six feet above lower levels by personal fall arrest systems, covers, or guardrail systems erected around the holes, (2) tripping in or stepping into or through holes (including skylights) by covers, and (3) objects falling through holes (including skylights) by covers. §1926.501(b)(4) **#18**

- ***Formwork and reinforcing steel***—Employees on the face of formwork or reinforcing steel must be protected from falling six feet or more to lower levels by personal fall arrest, safety net, or positioning device systems. §1926.501(b)(5)

- ***Ramps, runways, and other walkways***—Employees on ramps, runways, and other walkways must be protected from falling six feet or more to lower levels by guardrail systems. §1926.501(b)(6)

- ***Roofing work on low-slope roofs***—Except as otherwise provided in §1926.501(b), employees doing roofing activities on low-slope roofs, with unprotected sides and edges six feet or more above lower levels, must be protected from falling by a guardrail, safety net, or personal fall arrest system; or a combination of a warning line and guardrail system; warning line and safety net system; or warning line and personal fall arrest system; or warning line and safety monitoring system. Or, on roofs 50-feet or less wide (see Appendix A to subpart M of Part 1926), the use of a safety monitoring system alone (i.e. without the warning line system) is permitted. §1926.501(b)(10) **#21**

- ***Steep roofs***—Employees on steep roofs with unprotected sides and edges six feet or more above lower levels must be protected from falling by guardrail with toeboards, safety net, or personal fall arrest systems. §1926.501(b)(11) **#33**

- ***Precast concrete erection***—Employees engaged in the erection of precast concrete members (including, but not limited to the erection of wall panels, columns, beams, and floor and roof tees) and related operations such as grouting of precast concrete members, who are six feet or more above lower levels must be protected from falling by guardrail, safety net, or personal fall arrest systems, unless another provision in paragraph §1926.501(b) provides for an alternative fall protection measure. See §1926.501(b)(12) for exceptions.

- ***Residential construction***—Employees doing residential construction activities six feet or more above lower levels must be protected by a guardrail, safety net, or personal fall arrest system unless another provision in §1926.501(b) provides for an alternative fall protection measure. Exception: When an employer can demonstrate that it is infeasible or creates a greater hazard to use these systems, the employer must develop and implement a fall protection plan which meets the requirements of §1926.502(k). §1926.501(b)(13) **#15**

Note: See *Residential Construction—OSHA's Interim Fall Protection Compliance Guidelines* page 89 for other residential construction fall protection alternatives.

- ***Wall openings***—Employees working on, at, above, or near wall openings (including those with chutes attached) where the outside bottom edge of the wall opening is six feet or more above lower levels and the inside bottom edge of the wall opening is less than 39 inches above the walking/working surface, must be protected from falling by a guardrail, safety net, or a personal fall arrest system. §1926.501(b)(14) **#35**

- ***Walking/working surfaces not otherwise addressed***—Except as provided in §1926.500(a)(2) or in §1926.501(b)(1) through (b)(14), each employee on a walking/working surface six feet or more above lower levels must be protected from falling by a guardrail, safety net, or personal fall arrest system. §1926.501(b)(15) **#56**

- ***Protection from falling objects***—When employees are exposed to falling objects, employers must: ensure employees wear hard hats, and implement one of the measures in §1926.501(c).

Key Construction Regulation Summaries

Systems and criteria—General

Employers must provide and install all fall protection systems required by 29 CFR Subpart L—Fall protection, and must comply with all other pertinent requirements of Subpart L before employees begin the work that requires the fall protection. §1926.502(a)(2)

Systems and criteria—Guardrail systems

- The top edge height of top rails, or equivalent guardrail system members, must be 42 +/-3 inches above the walking/working level. When conditions warrant, the height of the top edge may exceed the 45-inch height, provided the guardrail system meets all other criteria of §1926.502(b)(1). **#89**

- Midrails, screens, mesh, intermediate vertical members, or equivalent intermediate structural members must be installed between the top edge of the guardrail and the walking/working surface when there is no wall or parapet wall at least 21 inches high. Other requirements for midrails, screens and mesh, intermediate members, and other structural members must also meet the requirements found in §1926.502(b)(2)(i) through (iv). **#94**

- Guardrail systems must be capable of withstanding, without failure, a force of at least 200 pounds applied within two inches of the top edge, in any outward or downward direction, at any point along the top edge. §1926.502(b)(3)

- When the 200 pound test load specified in paragraph §1926.502(b)(3) is applied in a downward direction, the top edge of the guardrail must not deflect to a height less than 39 inches above the walking/working level. Guardrail system components selected and constructed in accordance with §1926, Subpart M, Appendix B will be deemed to meet this requirement. §1926.502(b)(4)

- Top rails and midrails must be at least ¼ inch nominal diameter or thickness to prevent cuts and lacerations. If wire rope is used for top rails, it must be flagged at not more than six foot intervals with high-visibility material. §1926.502(b)(9)

- When guardrail systems are used around holes used as points of access (such as ladder-ways), they must be provided with a gate, or be so offset that a person cannot walk directly into the hole. §1926.502(b)(13)

Systems and criteria—Safety net systems

Safety nets must be installed as close as practicable under the walking/working surface on which employees are working, but in no case more than 30 feet below that level. When nets are used on bridges, the potential fall area from the walking/working surface to the net must be unobstructed. §1926.502(c)(1)

Systems and criteria—Personal fall arrest

- Horizontal lifelines must be designed, installed, and used, under the supervision of a qualified person, as part of a complete personal fall arrest system. The system must maintains a safety factor of at least two. §1926.502(d)(8)

- Lifelines must be protected against being cut or abraded. §1926.502(d)(11)

- Anchorages used for attachment of personal fall arrest equipment must be independent of any anchorage being used to support or suspend platforms and capable of supporting at least 5,000 pounds per employee attached, or must be designed, installed, and used: (1) as part of a complete personal fall arrest system which maintains a safety factor of at least two, and (2) under the supervision of a qualified person. §1926.502(d)(15)

- Personal fall arrest systems, when stopping a fall, must meet the requirements in §1926.502(d)(16)(i) through (v).

- The attachment point of a body belt must be located in the center of the wearer's back. The attachment point of a body harness must be located in the center of the wearer's back near shoulder level, or above the wearer's head. §1926.502(d)(17)

- Personal fall arrest systems must be inspected prior to each use for wear, damage, and other deterioration. Defective components must be removed from service. §1926.502(d)(21)

- Personal fall arrest systems must not be attached to guardrails, nor can they be attached to hoists except as specified in other subparts of the construction regulations. §1926.502(d)(23)

Systems and criteria—Warning lines

- Warning lines must be erected around all sides of a roof work area and must meet the requirements in §1926.502(f)(1)(i) through (iv).

- Warning lines must consist of ropes, wires, or chains, and supporting stanchions erected in accordance with §1926.502(f)(2)(i) through (v).

- Mechanical equipment on roofs must be used or stored only in areas where employees are protected by a warning line, guardrail, or personal fall arrest system. §1926.502(f)(4)

Systems and criteria—Safety monitoring

Safety monitoring systems (see §1926.501(b)(10) and §1926.502(k)) and their use must comply with the provisions at §1926.502(h)(i) through (v).

Systems and criteria—Covers

- Covers located in roadways and vehicular aisles must be capable of supporting, without failure, at least twice the maximum axle load of the largest vehicle expected to cross over the cover. All covers, other than covers located in roadways and vehicular aisles

Key Construction Regulation Summaries

(see §1926.502(i)(1)) must be capable of supporting, without failure, at least twice the weight of employees, equipment, and materials that may be imposed on the cover at any one time. §1926.502(i)(2)

- When installed, all covers must be secured so as to prevent accidental displacement by the wind, equipment, or employees. §1926.502(i)(3)   **#83**

- All covers must be color coded or they must be marked with the word "HOLE" or "COVER" to provide warning of the hazard. This provision does not apply to cast iron manhole covers or steel grates used on streets or roadways. §1926.502(i)(4)

Systems and criteria—Protection from falling objects

During roofing work: (1) materials and equipment must not be stored within six feet of a roof edge unless guardrails are erected at the edge, and (2) materials which are piled, grouped, or stacked near a roof edge must be stable and self-supporting. §1926.502(j)(7)

Training requirements—Training program

- Employers must provide a training program for employees who might be exposed to fall hazards. The program must train employees to recognize the hazards of falling and the procedures to be followed in order to minimize those hazards. §1926.503(a)(1)   **#11**

- Employers must assure that each employee has been trained, as necessary, by a competent person qualified in the areas outlined in §1926.503(a)(2)(i) through (vii). **#72**

Training requirements—Certification of training

Employers must verify compliance with §1926.503(a) by preparing a written certification record. The written certification record must contain the name or other identity of the employee trained, the date(s) of the training, and the signature of the person who conducted the training or the signature of the employer. If the employer relies on training conducted by another employer or completed prior to the effective date of this section, the certification record must indicate the date the employer determined the prior training was adequate rather than the date of actual training. The latest training certification be maintained. §1926.503(b)   **#67**

Training requirements—Retraining

When employers have reason to believe that any affected employee who has already been trained does not have the understanding and skill required by §1926.503(a), they must retrain that employee. Circumstances where retraining is required include, but are not limited to, situations where: (1) changes in the workplace render previous training obsolete, (2) changes in the types of fall protection systems or equipment to be used render previous training obsolete, or (3) inadequacies in an affected employee's knowledge or use of fall protection systems or equipment indicate that the employee has not retained the requisite understanding or skill. §1926.503(c)   **#68**

Cranes, derricks, hoists, elevators, and conveyors—§1926, Subpart N

Cranes and derricks—General requirements

- Employers must comply with the manufacturer's specifications and limitations applicable to the operation of any and all cranes and derricks. Where manufacturer's specifications are not available, the limitations assigned to the equipment must be based on the determinations of a qualified engineer competent in this field and such determinations will be appropriately documented and recorded. §1926.550(a)(1)

    - Attachments used with cranes must not exceed the capacity, rating, or scope recommended by the manufacturer.

- Rated load capacities, and recommended operating speeds, special hazard warnings, or instruction, must be conspicuously posted on all equipment. Instructions or warnings must be visible to operators while they are at their control station. §1926.550(a)(2)

- Employers must designate a competent person who must inspect all machinery and equipment prior to each use, and during use, to make sure it is in safe operating condition. Any deficiencies must be repaired, or defective parts replaced, before continued use. §1926.550(a)(5)

- A thorough, annual inspection of the hoisting machinery must be made by a competent person, or by a government or private agency recognized by the U.S. Department of Labor. Employers must maintain a record of the dates and results of inspections for each hoisting machine and piece of equipment. §1926.550(a)(6)

- Wire rope must be taken out of service when any of the following conditions exist: §1926.550(a)(7)

    - In running ropes, six randomly distributed broken wires in one lay or three broken wires in one strand in one lay.

    - Wear of one-third the original diameter of outside individual wires. Kinking, crushing, bird caging, or any other damage resulting in distortion of the rope structure.

    - Evidence of any heat damage from any cause.

    - Reductions from nominal diameter of more than 1/64" for diameters up to and including 5/16", 1/32" for diameters 3/8" to and including 1/2", 3/64" for diameters 9/16" to and including 3/4", 1/16" for diameters 7/8" to 1 1/8" inclusive, 3/32" for diameters 1 1/4" to 1 1/2" inclusive.

    - In standing ropes, more than two broken wires in one lay in sections beyond end connections or more than one broken wire at an end connection.

- Wire rope safety factors must be in accordance with American National Standards Institute B 30.5-1968 or SAE J959-1966.

Key Construction Regulation Summaries

- Accessible areas within the swing radius of the rear of a crane's rotating superstructure must be barricaded to prevent employees from being struck or crushed by the crane. §1926.550(a)(9)

- All windows in cabs must be of safety glass, or equivalent, that introduces no visible distortion that will interfere with the safe operation of the machine. §1926.550(a)(12)

- Fuel tank filler pipe must be located or protected as to not allow spill or overflow to run onto the engine, exhaust, or electrical equipment of any machine being fueled. §1926.550(a)(14)

- An accessible fire extinguisher of 5BC rating, or higher, must be available at all operator stations or cabs of equipment. §1926.550(a)(14)(i)

- All fuels must be transported, stored, and handled to meet the rules of Part 1926, Subpart F. When fuel is transported by vehicles on public highways, Department of Transportation rules contained in 49 CFR Parts 177 and 393 are considered applicable. §1926.550(a)(14)(ii)

- Except where electrical distribution and transmission lines have been deenergized and visibly grounded at the point of work or where insulating barriers, not a part of or an attachment to the equipment or machinery, have been erected to prevent physical contact with the lines, equipment or machines must be operated proximate to power lines only in accordance with the requirements of §1926.550(a)(15)(i) through (vii).

- All employees must be kept clear of loads about to be lifted and of suspended loads. §1926.550(a)(19)

Cranes and derricks—Crawler, locomotive, and truck cranes

All crawler, truck, or locomotive cranes in use must meet the applicable requirements for design, inspection, construction, testing, maintenance and operation as prescribed in the ANSI B30.5-1968, *Safety Code for Crawler, Locomotive and Truck Cranes*. However, the written, dated, and signed inspection reports and records of the monthly inspection of critical items prescribed in section 5-2.1.5 of the ANSI standard are not required. Instead, employers must prepare a certification record which includes: the date the crane items were inspected; the signature of the person who inspected the crane items; and a serial number, or other identifier, for the crane inspected. The most recent certification record must be maintained on file until a new one is prepared. §1926.550(b)(2)   **#95**

Cranes and derricks—Crane or derrick suspended personnel platforms

- This standard applies to the design, construction, testing, use and maintenance of personnel platforms, and the hoisting of personnel platforms on the load lines of cranes or derricks. §1926.550(g)(1)(i)

- *General requirements*—The use of a crane or derrick to hoist employees on a personnel platform is prohibited, except when the erection, use, and dismantling of conventional means of reaching the worksite, such as a personnel hoist, ladder, stairway, aerial lift, elevating work platform or scaffold, would be more hazardous or is not possible because of structural design or worksite conditions. §1926.550(g)(2)

- *Cranes and derricks—Operational criteria*—Hoisting of the personnel platform must be performed in a slow, controlled, cautious manner with no sudden movements of the crane or derrick, or the platform, and must be accomplished in accordance with the criteria of §1926.550(g)(3)(i) through (ii).

- *Personnel platforms—Design criteria*—The personnel platform and suspension system must be designed by a qualified engineer or a qualified person competent in structural design and must meet the requirements of §1926.550(g)(4)(i) through (iv).

- *Trial lift, inspections, and proof testing*—A trial lift, with the unoccupied personnel platform loaded at least to the anticipated lift weight, must be made from ground level, or any other location where employees will enter the platform to each location at which the personnel platform is to be hoisted and positioned. This trial lift must be performed immediately prior to placing personnel on the platform. The operator must determine that all systems, controls and safety devices are activated and functioning properly; that no interferences exist; and that all configurations necessary to reach those work locations will allow the operator to remain under the 50 percent limit of the hoist's rated capacity. Materials and tools to be used during the actual lift can be loaded in the platform, as provided in §1926.550(g)(4)(iii)(D), and (E) for the trial lift. A single trial lift may be performed at one time for all locations that are to be reached from a single set up position. The lift must meet all the requirements of §1926.550(g)(5)(i) through (vi).

- *Work practices*—Employees must keep all parts of their body inside the platform during raising, lowering, and positioning. This provision does not apply to an occupant of the platform performing the duties of a signal person. Other work practices, found in §1926.550(g)(6)(i) through (viii) must be followed.

Motor vehicles, mechanized equipment, and marine operations (including forklifts)—§1926, Subpart O

Equipment—General requirements

- Heavy machinery, equipment, or parts thereof, which are suspended or held aloft by use of slings, hoists, or jacks must be substantially blocked or cribbed to prevent falling or shifting before employees are permitted to work under or between them. §1926.600(a)(3)(i)

- Bulldozer and scraper blades, end-loader buckets, dump bodies, and similar equipment, must be either fully lowered or blocked when being repaired or when not in use. All controls must be in a neutral position, with the motors stopped and brakes set, unless work being performed requires otherwise. §1926.600(a)(3)(i)

Key Construction Regulation Summaries

- Whenever equipment is parked, the parking brake must be set. Equipment parked on inclines must have the wheels chocked and the parking brake set. §1926.600(a)(3)(ii)

- All cab glass must be safety glass, or equivalent, that introduces no visible distortion affecting the safe operation of any machine covered by this subpart. §1926.600(a)(5)

- All equipment covered by 1926, Subpart O must comply with the requirements of §1926.550(a)(15) when working or being moved in the vicinity of power lines or energized transmitters. §1926.600(a)(6)

Motor vehicles—General requirements

- Employers can't use any motor vehicle equipment having an obstructed view to the rear unless: (1) the vehicle has a reverse signal alarm audible above the surrounding noise level, or (2) the vehicle is backed up only when an observer signals that it is safe to do so. §1926.601(b)(4)

- Vehicles used to transport employees must have seats firmly secured and adequate for the number of employees to be carried. §1926.601(b)(8)

- All vehicles in use must be checked at the beginning of each shift to assure that the following parts, equipment, and accessories are in safe operating condition and free of apparent damage that could cause failure while in use: service brakes, including trailer brake connections; parking system (hand brake); emergency stopping system (brakes); tires; horn; steering mechanism; coupling devices; seat belts; operating controls; and safety devices. §1926.601(b)(14)

  - All defects must be corrected before the vehicle is placed in service. These requirements also apply to equipment such as lights, reflectors, windshield wipers, defrosters, fire extinguishers, etc., where such equipment is necessary.

Earthmoving equipment

These rules apply to the following types of earthmoving equipment: scrapers, loaders, crawler or wheel tractors, bulldozers, off-highway trucks, graders, agricultural and industrial tractors, and similar equipment.

- Seat belts must be provided on all equipment covered by this section (earthmoving equipment) and must meet the requirements of the Society of Automotive Engineers, J386-1969, *Seat Belts for Construction Equipment*. Seat belts for agricultural and light industrial tractors must meet the seat belt requirements of Society of Automotive Engineers J333a-1970, *Operator Protection for Agricultural and Light Industrial Tractors*. §1926.602(a)(2)

- Seat belts and anchorages meeting the requirements of 49 CFR Part 571 (Department of Transportation, Federal Motor Vehicle Safety Standards) must be installed in all motor vehicles. §1926.602(a)(9)   **#65**

Excavating and other equipment

The safety requirements, ratios, or limitations applicable to machines or attachment usage covered in Power Crane and Shovel Associations Standards No. 1 and No. 2 of 1968, and No. 3 of 1969, must be complied with, and must apply to cranes, machines, and attachments under the OSHA construction regulations. §1926.602(b)(3)

Lifting and hauling equipment (including forklifts) (other than equipment covered under Subpart N—Cranes, and derricks).

Lift trucks, stackers, etc., must have the rated capacity clearly posted on the vehicle so as to be clearly visible to the operator. When auxiliary removable counterweights are provided by the manufacturer, corresponding alternate rated capacities also must be clearly shown on the vehicle. These ratings must not be exceeded. Lifting and hauling equipment must also meet all requirements of §1926.602(c)(1)(i) through (viii). **#46**

Powered industrial truck (forklift) training

Employers must ensure that each powered industrial truck operator is competent to operate a powered industrial truck safely, as demonstrated by the successful completion of the training and evaluation specified in §1910.178(l). §1926.602(d)

Access to barges

Unless employees can step safely to or from the wharf, float, barge, or river towboat, either a ramp, meeting the requirements of §1926.605(b)(1), or a safe walkway, must be provided. §1926.605(b)(2)

Excavations—§1926, Subpart P

Underground installations

- The estimated location of utility installations, such as sewer, telephone, fuel, electric, water lines, or any other underground installations that reasonably may be expected to be encountered during excavation work, must be determined prior to opening an excavation. §1926.651(b)(1)

- Utility companies or owners must be contacted within established or customary local response times, advised of the proposed work, and asked to establish the location of the utility underground installations prior to the start of actual excavation. When utility companies or owners cannot respond to requests within 24 hours (unless a longer period is required by state or local law), or cannot establish the exact location of installations, employers may proceed, provided they do so with caution, and provided detection equipment or other acceptable means to locate utility installations are used. §1926.651(b)(2)

- When excavation operations approach the estimated location of underground installations, the exact location of the installations must be determined by safe and acceptable means. §1926.651(b)(3)

Key Construction Regulation Summaries

- While the excavation is open, underground installations must be protected, supported or removed as necessary to safeguard employees. §1926.651(b)(4)

Access and egress

A stairway, ladder, ramp or other safe means of egress must be located in trench excavations that are four feet or more deep so as to require no more than 25 feet of lateral travel for employees. §1926.651(c)(2)   **#20**

Exposure to vehicular traffic

Employees exposed to public vehicular traffic must be provided with, and must wear, warning vests or other suitable garments marked with or made of reflectorized or high-visibility material. §1926.651(d)   **#100**

Exposure to falling loads

- No employee can be permitted underneath loads handled by lifting or digging equipment. Employees must be required to stand away from any vehicle being loaded or unloaded to avoid being struck by any spillage or falling materials. §1926.651(e)

- Operators may remain in the cabs of vehicles being loaded or unloaded when the vehicles are equipped, in accordance with §1926.601(b)(6), to provide adequate protection for the operator during loading and unloading operations. §1926.651(e)

Hazardous atmospheres

- In addition to the requirements set forth in §1926, Subparts D—Occupational health and environmental controls, and E—Personal protective equipment, to prevent exposure to harmful levels of atmospheric contaminants, and to assure acceptable atmospheric conditions, the following requirements apply: §1926.651(g)(1)(i) through (iv).

  - Where oxygen deficiency (atmospheres containing less than 19.5 percent oxygen), or a hazardous atmosphere exists or could reasonably be expected to exist, such as in excavations in landfill areas or excavations in areas where hazardous substances are stored nearby, the atmospheres in the excavation must be tested before employees enter excavations greater than four feet deep.

  - Adequate precautions must be taken to prevent employee exposure to atmospheres containing less than 19.5 percent oxygen and other hazardous atmospheres. These precautions include providing proper respiratory protection or ventilation in accordance with §1926, Subparts D—Occupational health and environmental controls, and E—Personal protective equipment respectively.

  - Adequate precaution must be taken, such as providing ventilation, to prevent employee exposure to an atmosphere containing a concentration of a flammable gas in excess of 20 percent of the lower flammable limit of the gas.

- When controls are used that are intended to reduce the level of atmospheric contaminants to acceptable levels, testing must be conducted as often as necessary to ensure that the atmosphere remains safe.

Protections from hazards associated with water accumulations

Employees must not work in excavations where there is accumulated water, or in excavations in which water is accumulating, unless adequate precautions have been taken to protect employees against the hazards posed by water accumulation. The precautions necessary to protect employees adequately vary with each situation, but could include special support or shield systems to protect from cave-ins, water removal to control the level of accumulating water, or use of a safety harness and lifeline. §1926.651(h)(1)

Stability of adjacent structures

- Where the stability of adjoining buildings, walls, or other structures is endangered by excavation operations, support systems such as shoring, bracing, or underpinning must be provided to ensure the stability of such structures for the protection of employees. §1926.651(i)(1)

- Sidewalks, pavements, and appurtenant structures must not be undermined unless a support system or another method of protection is provided to protect employees from the possible collapse of such structures. §1926.651(i)(3)

Protection of employees from loose rock or soil

- Adequate protection must be provided to protect employees from loose rock or soil that could pose a hazard by falling or rolling from an excavation face. Such protection must consist of scaling to remove loose material; installation of protective barricades at intervals as necessary on the face to stop and contain falling material; or other means that provide equivalent protection. §1926.651(j)(1)

- Employees must be protected from excavated or other materials or equipment that could pose a hazard by falling or rolling into excavations. Protection must be provided by placing and keeping such materials or equipment at least two feet from the edge of excavations, or by the use of retaining devices that are sufficient to prevent materials or equipment from falling or rolling into excavations, or by a combination of both if necessary. §1926.651(j)(2)   **#30**

Inspections

- Daily inspections of excavations, the adjacent areas, and protective systems must be made by a competent person for evidence of a situation that could result in possible cave-ins, indications of failure of protective systems, hazardous atmospheres, or other hazardous conditions.

    An inspection must be conducted by the company's competent person prior to the start of work and as needed throughout the shift. Inspections must also be made after every

Key Construction Regulation Summaries

rainstorm or other hazard increasing occurrence. These inspections are only required when employee exposure can be reasonably anticipated. §1926.651(k)(1)   **#24**

- Where the company's competent person finds evidence of a situation that could result in a possible cave-in, indications of failure of protective systems, hazardous atmospheres, or other hazardous conditions, exposed employees must be removed from the hazardous area until the necessary precautions have been taken to ensure their safety. §1926.651(k)(2)   **#66**

Protection of employees in excavations

- Each employee in an excavation must be protected from cave-ins by an adequate protective system designed in accordance with §1926.652(b) or (c) except when: (1) excavations are made entirely in stable rock, or (2) excavations are less than five feet deep and examination of the ground by a competent person provides no indication of a potential cave-in. §1926.652(a)(1)   **#4**

- Protective systems must have the capacity to resist, without failure, all loads that are intended or could reasonably be expected to be applied or transmitted to the system. §1926.652(a)(2)

Design of sloping and benching systems

- The slopes and configurations of sloping and benching systems must be selected and constructed by the employer or his designee and must be in accordance with the requirements of §1926.652(b)(1), (2), (3), or, (4). §1926.652(b)

Design of support systems, shield systems, and other protective systems

Designs of support systems, shield systems, and other protective systems must be selected and constructed by the employer or his designee and must be in accordance with the requirements of §1926.652(c)(1), (2), (3), or (4). §1926.652(c)

Installation and removal of support

Members of support systems must be securely connected together to prevent sliding, falling, kick outs, or other predictable failures and must meet the requirements of §1926.652(e).

Shield systems

Shield systems must not be subjected to loads exceeding those which the system was designed to withstand and must meet the requirements of §1926.652(g).

Concrete and masonry construction—§1926, Subpart Q

- All protruding reinforcing steel, onto and into which employees could fall, must be guarded to eliminate the hazard of impalement. §1926.701(b) **#29**

- A limited access zone must be established whenever a masonry wall is being constructed. The zone must conform to the requirements of §1926.706(a).

- All masonry walls over eight feet high must be adequately braced to prevent overturning and collapse unless the wall is adequately supported to prevent overturn or collapse. The bracing must remain in place until permanent supporting elements of the structure are in place. §1926.706(b).

Steel erection—§1926, Subpart R

Temporary flooring—skeleton steel construction in tiered buildings

- The derrick or erection floor must be solidly planked or decked over its entire surface except for access openings. Planking or decking of equivalent strength, must be of proper thickness to carry the working load. Planking must be not less than two inches thick full size undressed, and must be laid tight and secured to prevent movement. §1926.750(b)(1)(i)

- On buildings or structures not adaptable to temporary floors, and where scaffolds are not used, safety nets must be installed and maintained whenever the potential fall distance exceeds two stories or 25 feet. The nets must be hung with sufficient clearance to prevent contacts with the surface of structures below. §1926.750(b)(1)(ii)

- A safety railing of ½-inch wire rope or equal must be installed, approximately 42 inches high around the periphery of all temporary-planked or temporary metal-decked floors of tier buildings and other multifloored structures during structural steel assembly. §1926.750(b)(1)(iii)

- Where skeleton steel erection is being done, a tightly planked and substantial floor must be maintained within two stories or 30 feet, whichever is less, below and directly under that portion of each tier of beams on which any work is being performed, except when gathering and stacking temporary floor planks on a lower floor in preparation for transferring such planks for use on an upper floor. Where such a floor is not practicable, paragraph §1926.750(b)(1)(ii) applies. §1926.750(b)(2)(i)

- When gathering and stacking temporary floor planks, the planks must be removed successively, working toward the last panel of the temporary floor so that the work is always done from the planked floor. §1926.750(b)(2)(ii)

Key Construction Regulation Summaries

- When gathering and stacking temporary floor planks from the last panel, the employees assigned to the work must be protected by safety belts with safety lines attached to a catenary line or other substantial anchorage. §1926.750(b)(2)(iii)

Assembly

Tag lines must be used for controlling loads. §1926.751(d)

Demolition—§1926, Subpart T

Preparatory operations

- Prior to permitting employees to start demolition operations, your competent person must make an engineering survey of the structure to determine the condition of the framing, floors, and walls, and possibility of unplanned collapse of any portion of the structure. Any adjacent structure where employees may be exposed must also be similarly checked. The employer must have in writing evidence that such a survey has been performed. §1926.850(a)

- Where a hazard exists to employees falling through wall openings, the opening must be protected to a height of approximately 42 inches. §1926.850(g)

Chutes

Material must not be dropped to any point lying outside the exterior walls of the structure unless the area is effectively protected. §1926.852(a)

Stairways and ladders—§1926, Subpart X

General requirements

A stairway or ladder must be provided at all personnel points of access where there is a break in elevation of 19 inches or more, and no ramp, runway, sloped embankment, or personnel hoist is provided. §1926.1051(a) **#41**

Stairways—General

- Riser height and tread depth must be uniform within each flight of stairs, including any foundation structure used as one or more treads of the stairs. Variations in riser height or tread depth must not be over ¼-inch in any stairway system. §1926.1052(a)(3)

- Where doors or gates open directly on a stairway, a platform must be provided, and the swing of the door must not reduce the effective width of the platform to less than 20 inches. §1926.1052(a)(4)

- Slippery conditions on stairways must be eliminated before the stairways are used to reach other levels. §1926.1052(a)(7)

Stairways—Temporary service

- Except during stairway construction, foot traffic is prohibited on stairways with pan stairs where the treads and/or landings are to be filled in with concrete or other material at a later date, unless the stairs are temporarily fitted with wood or other solid material at least to the top edge of each pan. Such temporary treads and landings must be replaced when worn below the level of the top edge of the pan. §1926.1052(b)(1) **#97**

- Except during stairway construction, foot traffic is prohibited on skeleton metal stairs where permanent treads and/or landings are to be installed at a later date, unless the stairs are fitted with secured temporary treads and landings long enough to cover the entire tread and/or landing area. §1926.1052(b)(2)

Stairways—Stairrails and handrails

- Stairways having four or more risers or rising more than 30 inches, whichever is less, must be equipped with: (1) at least one handrail, and (2) one stairrail system along each unprotected side or edge. Note: When the top edge of a stairrail system also serves as a handrail, §1926.1052(c)(7) applies. §1926.1052(c)(1) **#19**

- Midrails, screens, mesh, intermediate vertical members, or equivalent intermediate structural members, must be provided between the top rail of the stairrail system and the stairway steps. §1926.1052(c)(4)

- Midrails, when used, must be located at a height midway between the top edge of the stairrail system and the stairway steps. §1926.1052(c)(4)(i)

- Screens or mesh, when used, must extend from the top rail to the stairway step, and along the entire opening between top rail supports. §1926.1052(c)(4)(ii)

- When intermediate vertical members, such as balusters, are used between posts, they must be not more than 19 inches apart. §1926.1052(c)(4)(iii)

- Other structural members, when used, must be installed such that there are no openings in the stairrail system that are more than 19 inches wide. §1926.1052(c)(4)(iv)

- Unprotected sides and edges of stairway landings must be provided with guardrail systems. Guardrail system criteria are contained in §1926, subpart M—Fall protection. §1926.1052(c)(12) **#75**

Ladders—General

The following requirements apply to all ladders as indicated, including job-made ladders. §1926.1053(a)

- Ladders must be capable of supporting the following loads without failure: §1926.1053(a)(1)

Key Construction Regulation Summaries

- Each self-supporting portable ladder: At least four times the maximum intended load, except that each extra-heavy-duty type 1A metal or plastic ladder must sustain at least 3.3 times the maximum intended load. The ability of a ladder to sustain the loads indicated here must be determined by applying or transmitting the requisite load to the ladder in a downward vertical direction. Ladders built and tested in conformance with the applicable provisions of §1926, Subpart X, Appendix A will be deemed to meet this requirement. §1926.1053(a)(1)(i)

- Each portable ladder that is not self-supporting: At least four times the maximum intended load, except that each extra-heavy-duty type 1A metal or plastic ladder must sustain at least 3.3 times the maximum intended load. The ability of a ladder to sustain the loads indicated in this paragraph must be determined by applying or transmitting the requisite load to the ladder in a downward vertical direction when the ladder is placed at an angle of 75½ degrees from the horizontal. Ladders built and tested in conformance with the applicable provisions of §1926, Subpart X, Appendix A will be deemed to meet this requirement. §1926.1053(a)(1)(ii)

- Each Fixed ladder: At least two loads of 250 pounds each, concentrated between any two consecutive attachments (the number and position of additional concentrated loads of 250 pounds each, determined from anticipated usage of the ladder, must also be included), plus anticipated loads caused by ice buildup, winds, rigging, and impact loads resulting from the use of ladder safety devices. Each step or rung must be capable of supporting a single concentrated load of a least 250 pounds applied in the middle of the step or rung. Ladders built in conformance with the applicable provisions of §1926, Subpart X, Appendix A will be deemed to meet this requirement. §1926.1053(a)(1)(iii)

- Ladder rungs, cleats, and steps must be parallel, level, and uniformly spaced when the ladder is in position for use. §1926.1053(a)(2)

- Rungs, cleats, and steps of:

  - Portable ladders (except as provided below) and fixed ladders (including individual-rung/step ladders) must be spaced not less than 10 inches apart, nor more than 14 inches apart, as measured between center lines of the rungs, cleats, and steps. §1926.1053(a)(3)(i)

  - Step stools must be not less than eight inches, nor more than 12 inches apart, as measured between center lines of the rungs, cleats, and steps. §1926.1053(a)(3)(ii)

  - The base section of extension trestle ladders must be not less than 8 inches nor more than 18 inches apart, as measured between center lines of the rungs, cleats, and steps. The rung spacing on the extension section of the extension trestle ladder must be not less than six nor more than 12 inches, as measured between center lines of the rungs, cleats, and steps. §1926.1053(a)(3)(iii)

- The side rails of through or side-step fixed ladders must extend 42 inches above the top of the access level or landing platform served by the ladder. For a parapet ladder, the access level must be the roof if the parapet is cut to permit passage through the parapet; if the parapet is continuous, the access level will be the top of the parapet. §1926.1053(a)(24)

Ladders—Use

The following requirements apply to the use of all ladders, including job-made ladders, except as otherwise indicated. §1926.1053(b)

- When portable ladders are used for access to an upper landing surface, the ladder side rails must extend at least three feet above the upper landing surface to which the ladder is used to gain access; or, when such an extension is not possible because of the ladder's length, then the ladder must be secured at its top to a rigid support that will not deflect, and a grasping device, such as a grabrail, must be provided to assist employees in getting on and off the ladder. In no case can the extension be such that ladder deflection under a load would, by itself, cause the ladder to slip off its support. §1926.1053(b)(1)   **#12**

- Ladders must be used only for the purpose for which they were designed. §1926.1053(b)(4)   **#48**

- Non-self-supporting ladders must be used at an angle such that the horizontal distance from the top support to the foot of the ladder is approximately ¼ of the working length of the ladder (the distance along the ladder between the foot and the top support). §1926.1053(b)(5)(i)

- Wood job-made ladders with spliced side rails must be used at an angle such that the horizontal distance is one-eighth the working length of the ladder. §1926.1053(b)(5)(ii)

- Fixed ladders must be used at a pitch no greater than 90 degrees from the horizontal, as measured to the back side of the ladder. §1926.1053(b)(5)(iii)

- Ladders must be used only on stable and level surfaces unless secured to prevent accidental displacement. §1926.1053(b)(6)   **#92**

- Ladders must not be used on slippery surfaces unless secured or provided with slip-resistant feet to prevent accidental displacement. Slip-resistant feet must not be used as a substitute for care in placing, lashing, or holding a ladder that is used on slippery surfaces including, but not limited to, flat metal or concrete surfaces that are constructed so they cannot be prevented from becoming slippery. §1926.1053(b)(7)

- Ladders placed in any location where they can be displaced by workplace activities or traffic, such as in passageways, doorways, or driveways, must be secured to prevent accidental displacement, or a barricade must be used to keep the activities or traffic away from the ladder. §1926.1053(b)(8)   **#80**

- The area around the top and bottom of ladders must be kept clear. §1926.1053(b)(9)

Key Construction Regulation Summaries

- The top or top step of a stepladder must not be used as a step. §1926.1053(b)(13)   **#57**

- Ladders must be inspected periodically by a competent person for visible defects and after any occurrence that could affect their safe use. §1926.1053(b)(15)

- Portable ladders with structural defects, such as, but not limited to, broken or missing rungs, cleats, or steps, broken or split rails, corroded components, or other faulty or defective components, must either be immediately marked in a manner that readily identifies them as defective, or be tagged with "Do Not Use" or similar language, and be withdrawn from service until repaired. §1926.1053(b)(16)   **#79**

- When going up or down a ladder, the user must face the ladder. §1926.1053(b)(20)

- Employees must not carry any object or load that could cause them to lose balance and fall. §1926.1053(b)(22)

Stairways and ladders—Training requirements

- Employers must provide a training program for each employee using ladders and stairways, as necessary. The program must enable each employee to recognize hazards related to ladders and stairways, and train each employee in the procedures to be followed to minimize these hazards. §1926.1060(a)   **#45**

- Employers must ensure that each employee has been trained by a competent person in the following areas, as applicable:

    - The nature of fall hazards in the work area. §1926.1060(a)(1)(i)

    - The correct procedures for erecting, maintaining, and disassembling the fall protection systems to be used. §1926.1060(a)(1)(ii)

    - The proper construction, use, placement, and care in handling of all stairways and ladders. §1926.1060(a)(1)(iii)

    - The maximum intended load-carrying capacities of ladders used. §1926.1060(a)(1)(iv)

    - The standards contained in §1926, Subpart X. §1926.1060(a)(1)(v)

- Retraining must be provided for each employee as necessary so that the employee maintains the understanding and knowledge acquired through compliance with this section. §1926.1060(b)

Asbestos—§1926.1101

Scope and application

- This section regulates asbestos exposure in all work as defined in 29 CFR 1910.12(b), including but not limited to the following: §1926.1101(a)

  - Demolition or salvage of structures where asbestos is present. §1926.1101(a)(1)

  - Removal or encapsulation of materials containing asbestos. §1926.1101(a)(2)

  - Construction, alteration, repair, maintenance, or renovation of structures, substrates, or portions thereof, that contain asbestos. §1926.1101(a)(3)

  - Installation of products containing asbestos. §1926.1101(a)(4)

  - Asbestos spill/emergency cleanup. §1926.1101(a)(5)

  - Transportation, disposal, storage, containment of and housekeeping activities involving asbestos or products containing asbestos, on the site or location at which construction activities are performed. §1926.1101(a)(6)

- Coverage under this standard is based on the nature of the work operation involving asbestos exposure. §1926.1101(a)(7)

- This section does not apply to asbestos-containing asphalt roof coatings, cements and mastics. §1926.1101(a)(8)

Regulated areas

All Class I, II and III asbestos work must be conducted within regulated areas. All other operations covered by this standard must be conducted within a regulated area where airborne concentrations of asbestos exceed, or there is a reasonable possibility they may exceed a PEL. Regulated areas must comply with the requirements of paragraphs (2), (3),(4) and (5) of §1926.1101(e).

Exposure assessments and monitoring

- Each employer who has a workplace or work operation where exposure monitoring is required under this section must perform monitoring to determine accurately the airborne concentrations of asbestos to which employees may be exposed. §1926.1101(f)(1)

- Each employer who has a workplace or work operation covered by this standard must ensure that a "competent person" conducts an exposure assessment immediately before or at the initiation of the operation to ascertain expected exposures during that operation or workplace. The assessment must be completed in time to comply with requirements which are triggered by exposure data or the lack of a "negative exposure assessment," and to provide information necessary to assure that all control systems planned are appropriate for that operation and will work properly. §1926.1101(f)(2)

Key Construction Regulation Summaries

Methods of compliance

- Employers must use the engineering controls and work practices in §1926.1101(g)(1) through (3) in all operations covered by the asbestos standard, regardless of the levels of exposure. §1926.1101(g)(1) **#99**

- In addition to the provisions of paragraphs §1926.1101(g)(1) and (2) of the asbestos rule, the engineering controls and work practices and procedures in:

    - Section 1926.1101(g)(4), (5), and (6) must be used when performing Class I asbestos work.

    - Section 1926.1101(g)(7) and (8) must be used when performing Class II asbestos work.

    - Section 1926.1101(g)(9) must be used when performing Class III asbestos work.

    - Section 1926.1101(g)(10) must be used when performing Class IV asbestos work.

Respiratory protection

- For employees who use respirators required by the asbestos rule, employers must provide respirators that comply with the requirements of §1926.1101(h). Respirators must be used during:

    - Class I asbestos work.

    - Class II asbestos work when asbestos-containing material (ACM) is not removed in a substantially intact state.

    - Class II and III asbestos work that is not performed using wet methods, except for removal of ACM from sloped roofs when a negative-exposure assessment has been conducted, and ACM is removed in an intact state.

    - Class II and III asbestos work for which a negative-exposure assessment has not been conducted.

    - Class III asbestos work when thermal system insulation (TSI) or surfacing ACM or presumed asbestos containing material (PACM) is being disturbed.

    - Class IV asbestos work performed within regulated areas where employees who are performing other work are required to use respirators.

    - Work operations covered by the asbestos rule for which employees are exposed above the TWA or excursion limit.

    - Emergencies.

- Employers must implement a respiratory protection program in accordance with 29 CFR 1910.134(b) through (d) (except (d)(1)(iii)), and (f) through (m), and the requirements of §1926.1101(h)(2)(ii).

- Employers must select the appropriate respirator from Table 1 of §1926.1101(h) and meet the requirements of §1926.1101(h)(3).

Protective clothing

Employers must provide and require the use of protective clothing, such as coveralls or similar whole-body clothing, head coverings, gloves, and foot coverings for any employee exposed to airborne concentrations of asbestos that exceed the TWA and/or excursion limit prescribed in §1926.1101(c), or for which a required negative exposure assessment is not produced, or for any employee performing Class I operations which involve the removal of over 25 linear or 10 square feet of TSI or surfacing ACM and PACM. §1926.1101(i)(1).

Hygiene facilities and practices for employees

- When performing Class I asbestos work involving over 25 linear or 10 square feet of TSI or surfacing ACM or PACM, employers must follow the requirements found in §1926.1101(j)(1).

- When performing Class I asbestos work involving less than 25 linear or 10 square feet of TSI or surfacing ACM or PACM, and for Class II and Class III asbestos work operations where exposures exceed a PEL, or where there is no negative exposures assessment produced before the operation, employers must follow the requirements found in §1926.1101(j)(2).

Communication of hazards—Duties of employers whose employees perform work subject to the asbestos rule in or adjacent to areas containing ACM and PACM

Building/facility owners whose employees perform work subject to the asbestos rule in or adjacent to areas containing ACM and PACM must comply with the provisions in §1926.1101(k)(3) to the extent applicable.

Communication of hazards—Signs

- Warning signs that demarcate the regulated area must be provided and displayed at each location where a regulated area is required to be established by §1926.1101(e). Signs must be posted at such a distance from a location that an employee may read the signs and take necessary protective steps before entering the area marked by the signs. §1926.1101(k)(7)(i)

- The warning signs required by paragraph §1926.1101(k)(7) must bear the following information:

DANGER, ASBESTOS
CANCER AND LUNG DISEASE HAZARD
AUTHORIZED PERSONNEL ONLY

Key Construction Regulation Summaries

- In addition, where the use of respirators and protective clothing is required in the regulated area, the warning signs must include the following:

    RESPIRATORS AND PROTECTION CLOTHING
    ARE REQUIRED IN THIS AREA

- Employers must ensure that employees working in and contiguous to regulated areas comprehend the warning signs required to be posted by §1926.1101(k)(7)(i). Means to ensure employee comprehension may include the use of foreign languages, pictographs and graphics. §1926.1101(k)(7)(iii)

Housekeeping—Waste disposal

Asbestos waste, scrap, debris, bags, containers, equipment, and contaminated clothing consigned for disposal must be collected and disposed of in sealed, labeled, impermeable bags or other closed, labeled, impermeable containers except in roofing operations, where the procedures specified in §1926.1101(g)(8)(ii) apply. §1926.1101(l)(2)

Competent person

On all construction worksites covered by the asbestos regulation, employers must designate a competent person. The competent person must have the qualifications and authorities for ensuring worker safety and health required by §1926, Subpart C—General Safety and Health Provisions for Construction. §1926.1101(o)(1)

Summaries of Key OSHA General Industry (29 CFR Part 1910) Regulations Construction Companies are Frequently Cited for

OSHA does not use the general industry standards (29 CFR 1910) to cite construction companies (SIC codes 15, 16, and 17) engaged in construction activities. However, there are cases where construction companies receive 1910 citations. It is usually when an employee is in a general industry setting such as a vehicle maintenance facility, metal fabrication shop, or supply yard and doing general industry type activities.

The following 1910 rules are those most frequently referenced in citations received by construction companies. The rules are given in the order of the most frequent violations.

Protection of open-sided floors, platforms, and runways —§1910.23(c)(1)

Every open-sided floor or platform 4 feet or more above adjacent floor or ground level must be guarded by a standard railing (or the equivalent as specified in paragraph (e)(3) of this section) on all open sides except where there is entrance to a ramp, stairway, or fixed ladder. The railing must be provided with a toeboard wherever, beneath the open sides: (1) persons can pass, (2) there is moving machinery, or (3) there is equipment with which falling materials could create a hazard.

Vehicle-mounted elevating and rotating work platforms— Extensible and articulating boom platforms—§1910.67(c)(2)

- Lift controls must be tested each day prior to use to determine they are in safe working condition.

- Only trained employees can operate an aerial lift.

- A body belt must be worn and a lanyard attached to the boom or basket when working from an aerial lift.

- Belting off to an adjacent pole, structure, or equipment while working from an aerial lift is not be permitted.

- Employees must always stand firmly on the floor of the basket, and must not sit or climb on the edge of the basket or use planks, ladders, or other devices for a work position.

- Boom and basket load limits specified by the manufacturer must not be exceeded.

- The brakes must be set, and outriggers, when used, must be positioned on pads or a solid surface.

- Wheel chocks must be installed before using an aerial lift on an incline.

- An aerial lift truck may not be moved when the boom is elevated in a working position with men in the basket unless the equipment is specifically designed for this type of operation.

- Articulating boom and extensible boom platforms, primarily designed as personnel carriers, must have both platform (upper) and lower controls.

    - Upper controls must be in or beside the platform within easy reach of the operator.

    - Lower controls must provide for overriding the upper controls.

    - Controls must be plainly marked as to their function.

    - Lower level controls must not be operated unless permission has been obtained from the employee in the lift, except in the case of an emergency.

- Climbers must not be worn while working from an aerial lift.

- The insulated portion of an aerial lift must not be altered in any manner that might reduce its insulating value.

Personal protective equipment—Application—§1910.132(a)

Protective equipment—including personal protective equipment for eyes, face, head, and extremities—protective clothing, respiratory devices, and protective shields and barriers, must be provided, used, and maintained in a sanitary and reliable condition wherever it is necessary by reason of hazards of processes or environment, chemical hazards, radiological hazards, or mechanical irritants encountered in a manner capable of causing injury or impairment in the function of any part of the body through absorption, inhalation or physical contact.

Personal protective equipment—Hazard assessment and equipment selection—§1910.132(d)(1)

Employers must assess the workplace to determine if hazards are present, or are likely to be present, requiring using personal protective equipment (PPE). If such hazards are present, or likely to be present, employers must:

- Select, and ensure employees use, the types of PPE that will protect them from the hazards identified in the hazard assessment.

- Talk to affected employees about PPE selection decisions.

Key General Industry Regulation Summaries

- Select PPE that properly fits affected employees.

Personal protective equipment—Eye and face protection—§1910.133(a)(1)

Employers must ensure that each affected employee uses appropriate eye or face protection when exposed to eye or face hazards from flying particles, molten metal, liquid chemicals, acids or caustic liquids, chemical gases or vapors, or potentially injurious light radiation.

The control of hazardous energy (lockout/tagout)—§1910.147(c)(1), (4), (6), & (7)

- Employers must establish a program consisting of energy control procedures, employee training, and periodic inspections to ensure that before any employee performs any servicing or maintenance on a machine or equipment where the unexpected energizing start up or release of stored energy could occur and cause injury, the machine or equipment must be isolated from the energy source, and rendered inoperative.

- Procedures must be developed, documented, and utilized for the control of potentially hazardous energy when employees are engaged in the activities covered by this section.

  Employers need not document the required procedure for a particular machine or equipment, when all of the elements found in the exception at §1910.147(c)4 exist.

- Employers must conduct a periodic inspection of the energy control procedure at least annually to ensure that the procedure and the requirements of this standard are being followed.

- Employers must provide training to ensure that the purpose and function of the energy control program are understood by employees and that the knowledge and skills required for the safe application, usage, and removal of the energy controls are acquired by employees. The training must include the requirements of §1910.147(c)(7).

Electrical—General requirements—§1910.303(g)(2)

- Except as required or permitted elsewhere in the regulations, live parts of electric equipment operating at 50 volts or more must be guarded against accidental contact by approved cabinets or other forms of approved enclosures, or by:

  - Locating the equipment in a room, vault, or similar enclosure accessible only to qualified persons.

  - Erecting suitable, permanent, and substantial partitions or screens so arranged that only qualified persons will have access to the space within reach of the live parts.

- Locating on a suitable balcony, gallery, or platform so elevated and arranged as to exclude unqualified persons.

- Elevating eight feet or more above the floor or other working surface.

• In locations where electric equipment would be exposed to physical damage, enclosures or guards must be arranged and strong enough to prevent such damage.

• Entrances to rooms and other guarded locations containing exposed live parts must be marked with conspicuous warning signs forbidding unqualified persons to enter.

Electrical—Wiring design & protection—§1910.304(f)(4)

The path to ground from circuits, equipment, and enclosures must be permanent and continuous.

Electrical—Identification, splices, and terminations—§1910.305(g)(2)

• A conductor of a flexible cord or cable that is used as a grounded conductor or an equipment grounding conductor must be distinguishable from other conductors. Types SJ, SJO, SJT, SJTO, S, SO, ST, and STO must be durably marked on the surface with the type designation, size, and number of conductors.

• Flexible cords must be used only in continuous lengths without splice or tap. Hard service flexible cords No. 12 or larger may be repaired if spliced so that the splice retains the insulation, outer sheath properties, and usage characteristics of the cord being spliced.

• Flexible cords must be connected to devices and fittings so that strain relief is provided which will prevent pull from being directly transmitted to joints or terminal screws.

Electrical—Lockout and tagging— §1910.333(b)(2)

While any employee is exposed to contact with parts of fixed electric equipment or circuits which have been deenergized, the circuits energizing the parts must be locked out or tagged or both in accordance with the requirements of this paragraph. The requirements must be followed in the order in which they are presented (i.e., paragraph (b)(2)(i) first, then paragraph (b)(2)(ii), etc.).

Other Requirements Frequently Cited

These citations include violations of the General Duty Clause (Section 5(a)(1) of the Occupational Safety and Health Act), the posting and recordkeeping requirements of 29 CFR Parts 1903—Inspections, citations and proposed penalties, and the requirements of 29 CFR Part 1904—Recording and reporting occupational injuries and illnesses.

General Duty Clause—5(a)(1)

Hazardous conditions or practices not covered in an OSHA standard may be covered under Section 5(a)(1) of the Occupational Safety and Health Act of 1970. This section is referred to as the General Duty Clause and says:

> "Each employer shall furnish to each of his employees employment and a place of employment which is free from recognized hazards that are causing or are likely to cause death or serious physical harm to his employees."

OSHA cites the General Duty Clause in many of its enforcement actions when:

- The OSHA inspector does not have a regulation to reference but sees a recognized hazard that is causing or likely to cause death or serious physical harm to employees.

- A standard exists, but it is clear the hazard warrants additional precautions beyond what the current safety standard requires.

- The hazard still exists for the employee even after the employer has complied with a particular OSHA standard.

OSHA's recent action on ergonomic hazards in the workplace is a good example of General Duty Clause application in situations where a standard does not currently exist. There are no construction standards governing job or work station design to reduce or prevent cumulative trauma disorders or other injuries. However, OSHA has cited companies under the General Duty Clause for failing to address ergonomic hazards in the workplace.

OSHA has also issued General Duty Clause citations on other occasions where a safety standard was not apparent or did not exist. Citations have been issued for lack of training, failure to have additional safety or alarm equipment to detect or warn of chemical leaks, and failure to provide safe locations or safe access to valves or other instruments necessary to an employee's job.

Although OSHA does not cite employees, the OSH Act says in 5(b) that each employee shall comply with occupational safety and health standards and all rules, regulations, and orders issued pursuant to the Act which are applicable to his/her own actions and conduct.

There were 319 citations issued in FY 99/00 for violations of the General Duty Clause.

When can OSHA give you a General Duty Clause citation?

The Occupational Safety and Health Review Commission (OSHRC), and court precedent, has established that the following elements are necessary to prove a violation of the General Duty Clause:

- You fail to keep a jobsite free of a hazard to which your employees were exposed. A hazard is a danger which threatens physical harm to your employees.

- You recognized the hazard.

- The hazard was causing or was likely to cause death or serious physical harm.

- There was a feasible and useful method to correct the hazard.

OSHA inspectors can only use the General Duty Clause within the guidelines set forth in OSHA's Field Inspection Reference Manual (FIRM). This manual (OSHA Instruction CPL 2.103) is an inspector's guide for conducting inspections and issuing citations.

Inspections, citations and proposed penalties—Part 1903

- Employers must post and keep posted a notice or notices, furnished by OSHA, informing employees of the protections and obligations provided for in the OSH Act of 1970.

- Notices must be posted in a conspicuous place where notices to employees are customarily posted.

- If your state has a similar requirement for a poster informing employees of their protections and obligations, posting the state poster constitutes compliance with this requirement.

- Any citation received from OSHA must be posted at or near each place an alleged violation referred to in the citation occurred. The citation must be posted upon receipt and remain posted until the violation has been corrected, or for three working days, whichever is longer.

- If it is not possible to post the citation at or near each place of the alleged violation, the citation can be posted where all affected employees can see it. For example, where employees are engaged in activities in different locations, the citation may be posted at the location to which employees report each day.

- Notices of de minimis violations need not be posted.

Other Requirements Frequently Cited

Abatement verification—Part 1903.19

- OSHA's inspections are intended to result in the abatement of violations of the OSH Act. Section 1903.19 of the OSHA rules gives the procedures OSHA will use to ensure citations are abated. This section only applies to employers who receive a citation for a violation.

- *Abatement* means the action you take to comply with a cited rule or to eliminate a recognized hazard identified by OSHA during an inspection.

- Within 10 calendar days after the abatement date, you must certify to OSHA that each cited violation has been abated unless, within 24 hours, the OSHA inspector observes you fixing the problem and notes this in the citation.

- The employers certification of abatement must include, for each violation: (1) date and method of abatement, and (2) a statement that affected employees and their representatives have been informed of the abatement.

- You must submit to OSHA, documents demonstrating that abatement is complete for each willful or repeat violation and for any serious violation indicated in the citation that such abatement documentation is required.

- OSHA may require you to submit an abatement plan for each cited violation (except an other-than-serious) when the time permitted for abatement exceeds 90 calendar days.
    - Employers who are required to submit a plan may also be required to submit periodic progress reports.

- You must inform affected employees and their representative(s) about abatement activities by posting a copy of each document submitted to OSHA or a summary of the document near the place where the violation occurred. Where such postings do not effectively inform employees about abatement activities other methods must be used as outlined in the OSHA rule.

- For serious, repeat, and willful violations involving movable equipment, you must attach a warning tag or a copy of the citation to the operating controls or to the cited component of equipment that is moved within the worksite or between worksites.
    - You must use a warning tag that properly warns employees about the nature of the violation involving the equipment and identifies the location of the citation issued.
    - If the violation has not already been abated, a warning tag or copy of the citation must be attached to the equipment: (1) for hand-held equipment, immediately after you receive the citation, and (2) for non-hand-held equipment, prior to moving the equipment within or between worksites.

- For the construction industry, a tag that is designed and used in accordance with 29 CFR 1926.20(b)(3) and 1926.200(h) is deemed by OSHA to meet the requirements.

- You must assure that the tag or copy of the citation attached to moveable equipment is not altered, defaced, or covered by other material.

- You must assure that the tag or copy of the citation attached to moveable equipment remains attached until:

  - The violation has been abated and all abatement verification documents required by this rule have been submitted to OSHA.

  - The cited equipment has been permanently removed from service or is no longer within your control.

  - The Occupational Safety and Health Review Commission issues a final order vacating the citation.

Recording and reporting occupational injuries and illnesses—Part 1904

The Occupational Safety and Health (OSH) Act of 1970 requires covered employers to prepare and maintain records of occupational injuries and illnesses. The Bureau of Labor Statistics of the U. S. Department of Labor is responsible for administering the recordkeeping system established by the Act. The OSH Act and recordkeeping regulations in 29 CFR 1904 provide specific recording and reporting requirements which comprise the framework of the OSHA recording system. The following points provide an overview of the system.

Log and summary of occupational injuries and illnesses—§1904.2(a)

- If you have 11 or more employees (at any one time in the previous calendar year) you must maintain a log and summary of all recordable injuries and illnesses resulting in a fatality, hospitalization, lost workdays, medical treatment (other than first aid), job transfer or termination, loss of consciousness or restriction of work or motion. Each recordable event must be entered in the log and summary no later than six working days after receiving information that a recordable case has occurred.

- OSHA Form 200, or an equivalent form, shall be used to record the information. The log and summary must be completed in the detail provided in the form and instructions on the OSHA Form 200.

Recording and reporting occupational injuries and illnesses—Log copy—§1904.2(b)(2)

At each of the employer's establishments, there must be available a copy of the log which reflects separately the injury and illness experience of that establishment complete and current to a date within 45 calendar days.

Employees not associated with fixed establishments

An establishment is considered a single physical location where business is conducted or where services or industrial operations are performed. Some employees are subject to com-

Other Requirements Frequently Cited

mon supervision, but do not report or work at a fixed establishment regularly. These employees are engaged in physically dispersed activities that occur in construction, installation, repair, or services operations. Records for these employees should be located as follows: (1) records may be kept at the field office or mobile base of operation, or (2) records may also be kept at an established central location. If the records are kept centrally, the address and telephone number of the place where the records are kept must be available at the worksite, and there must be someone available at the central location during normal business hours to provide information from the records.

Recording and reporting occupational injuries and illnesses—Supplementary record—§1904.4

In addition to the log of occupational injuries and illnesses provided for under §1904.2, each employer must have available for inspection at each establishment within six working days after receiving information that a recordable case has occurred, a supplementary record for each occupational injury or illness for that establishment. The record must be completed in the detail prescribed in the instructions accompanying Occupational Safety and Health Administration Form OSHA No. 101. Workmen's compensation, insurance, or other reports are acceptable alternative records if they contain the information required by Form OSHA No. 101. If no acceptable alternative record is maintained for other purposes, Form OSHA No. 101 must be used or the necessary information must be otherwise maintained. §1904.4

Annual summary—1904.5(a)

- You must post an annual summary of occupational injuries and illnesses for each workplace/worksite. The summary must consist of a copy of the year's totals from the form OSHA No. 200 and the following information from that form:

    - Calendar year covered.

    - Company name.

    - Establishment name and address.

    - Certification signature, title, and date.

- A form OSHA 200 must be used in presenting the summary.

- If no injuries or illnesses occurred in the year, zeros must be entered on the totals line, and the form must be posted.

Annual summary—1904.5(c)

Each employer, or the employers representative who supervises the preparation of the log and summary of occupational injuries and illnesses, must certify that the annual summary is true and complete.

Access to records—1904.7

(a) Each employer shall provide, upon request, records provided for §§1904.2, §1904.4, and §1904.5, for inspection and copying by any representative of the Secretary of Labor for the purpose of carrying out the provisions of the Act, and by representatives of the Secretary of Health, Education, and Welfare during any investigation under section 20(b) of the act, or by any representative of a State accorded jurisdiction for occupational safety and health inspections or for statistical compilation under sections 18 and 24 of the Act.

(b) (1) The log and summary of all recordable occupational injuries and illnesses (OSHA No. 200) (the log) provided for in §1904.2 shall, upon request, be made available by the employer to any employee, former employee, and to their representatives for examination and copying in a reasonable manner and at reasonable times. The employee, former employee, and their representatives shall have access to the log for any establishment in which the employee is or has been employed.

(b)(2) Nothing in this section shall be deemed to preclude employees and employee representatives from collectively bargaining to obtain access to information relating to occupational injuries and illnesses in addition to the information made available under this section.

(b)(3) Access to the log provided under this section shall pertain to all logs retained under the requirements of §1904.6.

Reporting of fatality or multiple hospitalization incidents—1904.8

- Within eight hours after the death of any employee from a work-related incident, or the in-patient hospitalization of three or more employees as a result of a work-related incident, the employer of any employees so affected shall orally report the fatality/multiple hospitalization by telephone or in person to the Area Office of the Occupational Safety and Health Administration (OSHA), U.S. Department of Labor, that is nearest to the site of the incident, or by using the OSHA toll-free central telephone number 1-800-321-OSHA (6742).

    - This requirement applies to each such fatality or hospitalization of three or more employees which occurs within thirty (30) days of an incident.

- Exception: If you do not learn of a reportable incident at the time it occurs and the incident would otherwise be reportable under §1904.8(a) and (b), you must make the report within eight hours of the time the incident is reported to any agent or employee of the employer.

- Each report required by this section must relate the following information: establishment name, location of the incident, time of the incident, number of fatalities or hospitalized employees, contact person, phone number, and a brief description of the incident.

Other Requirements Frequently Cited

Annual OSHA injury and illness survey of ten or more employees—1904.17

- Most U.S. employers must keep records of occupational injuries and illnesses their workers experience. This rule clarifies OSHA's authority to request employers mail or electronically transmit that data directly to the agency. The rule amends 29 CFR Part 1904—Recording and reporting occupational injuries and illnesses.

- Each employer must, upon receipt of OSHA's Annual Survey Form, report the number of workers employed and number of hours worked for periods designated in the form.

- Reports must be sent to OSHA by mail or other means described in the survey within 30 calendar days, or the time stated in the survey, whichever is longer.

- Employers exempted from keeping injury and illness records under §§1904.15 and 1904.16 must maintain injury and illness records required by §§1904.2 and 1904.4, and make Survey Reports upon notification in writing by OSHA, in advance of the year for which injury and illness records will be required, that the employer has been selected to participate in an information collection.

OSHA Special Emphasis and Focused Programs

Crystalline Silica—OSHA's Special Emphasis Program

The Occupational Safety and Health Administration (OSHA) is conducting a national special emphasis program for crystalline silica. The program includes extensive employer and worker outreach education, and inspections, to reduce the potential threat of silicosis. Silicosis is a disabling and sometimes fatal disease.

The National Institute for Occupational Safety and Health (NIOSH) has estimated that two million workers in the U.S. are exposed annually to crystalline silica. Workers are especially at risk when sandblasting, drilling, or tunneling. OSHA wants to ensure they are protected as much as possible.

The special emphasis program will apply to all workplaces under OSHA's jurisdiction in general industry, construction, and maritime sectors.

Crystalline silica is the basic component of sand, quartz and granite rock. Activities that can generate airborne crystalline silica dust include: abrasive blasting, rock drilling, foundry work, grinding, stone cutting, mining and concrete drilling or cutting. Inhalation of airborne crystalline silica can lead to silicosis, a disabling, progressive, and sometimes fatal disease involving scarring of the lungs. About 300 deaths are attributed to silicosis each year. Inhaling silica dust is also associated with other diseases such as tuberculosis and lung cancer.

The program contains an element allowing for construction focused inspections (see page 80) on sites where silica is not controlled effectively. Inspectors will limit their inspections at sites that have implemented an effective and ongoing silicosis prevention program.

Elements of an effective silicosis prevention program may include:

- Ongoing personal air monitoring.
- Ongoing medical surveillance, training, and crystalline silica information for workers.
- Availability of air and medical surveillance data to workers.
- An effective respiratory protection program.
- Hygiene facilities.
- Appropriate recordkeeping.
- Personal exposures below the permissible exposure limit (PEL) or an abatement program that provides interim worker protection.
- A safety and health program addressing overexposure to crystalline silica.

- Regulated areas.

OSHA standards that may be referenced on an OSHA citation as part of crystalline silica enforcement include those listed in Table 1.

Table 2 lists Standard Industrial Classification Codes (SIC) where some sampling has been conducted. The table lists: (1) where over exposures have been found and documented, and (2) where exposures were not found. The list is only those SIC Codes that were monitored and samplings taken. It is not a list of the only SIC Codes inspectors will be looking at. Silica dust can be generated at any construction project.

For help in developing a silicosis prevention program, employers can contact their local OSHA Consultation Service for free guidance and assistance.

Table 1—List of standards that may, under appropriate inspection conditions, be cited for crystalline silica overexposure under the Special Emphasis Program for Silicosis

OSHA Requirement	Construction Standard
Respiratory protection	1926.103
Permissible exposure limit and controls	1926.55 & .57
Accident prevention & warning signs	1926.200
Access to employee exposure and medical records	1926.33
OSHA 200 forms	1904, 1926.22
Hygiene	1926.27 & .51
General PPE	1926.28, 95, 100-105
Hazard communication	1926.59
Safety and health program	1926.20
General training	1926.21

Table 2—Standard Industrial Classification Codes (SIC) where crystalline silica overexposures have been documented and where overexposures were not found

SIC Codes where overexposures to crystalline silica dust have been documented	SIC Codes where sampling has been conducted for crystalline silica dust during the previous three years and overexposures were not found
1542 Nonresidential construction	1611 Highway and street construction
1622 Bridge, tunnel, and elevated highway construction	1771 Concrete work
1629 Heavy construction	1793 Glass and glazing work
1721 Painting and paper hanging	1794 Excavation work
1741 Masonry and other stone work	1795 Wrecking and demolition
1799 Special trades contractors	

Special Emphasis and Focused Programs

Lead in Construction—OSHA's Special Emphasis Program

OSHA's CPL 2.105 establishes a nationally directed Special Emphasis Program (SEP) for programmed health inspections of lead in construction operations.

Background

Over the past several years OSHA inspections have documented elevated blood lead levels in construction workers. The source of the exposure is from the cutting, welding, grinding, and/or abrasive blasting on steel surfaces such as bridges and tanks that are coated with lead-bearing paints. In response, several state plan states, area offices, and regions have developed their own local emphasis programs to address this hazard in the construction industry.

OSHA therefore, has determined that an increased uniform OSHA enforcement presence is warranted at work sites where such exposures occur.

Procedures

Inspections under this special emphasis program will be scheduled and conducted under the following priority:

Referrals

For states that have enacted mandatory reporting of blood lead, the area or regional OSHA office will attempt to obtain the blood lead data where possible. Employers with worker blood lead levels above 40 micro-grams/100 grams of whole blood shall be targeted for inspection provided the worker can be identified with an employer.

Any means to determine when construction activities involve worker exposure to hazards associated with lead during abrasive blasting, sanding, cutting, burning, welding, painting, etc. of steel structures coated with lead contaminated paints, or during any other disturbance of lead containing materials shall be used. All compliance officers will be instructed to be on the lookout for construction activities where there is a potential for exposure to lead. Such activities can include, but are not limited to:

- Residential remodeling.
- Petroleum tank repainting.
- Indoor and outdoor industrial maintenance* and renovation.
- Commercial and institutional remodeling.
- Highway and railroad bridge repainting and rehabilitation.
- Lead joint work on cast iron soil pipes.
- Repair and removal of water lines.

- Water tank repainting and demolition.
- Highway and railroad bridge demolition.
- Housing lead abatement projects.
- Electric transmission and communication tower maintenance.*
- Electrical cable splicing and resplicing.
- Installation of terne roofing.
- Elevator cable babbitting.*
- Underground storage tank demolition.
- Stained glass window removal and repair.
- Mineral wool insulation with lead contamination.*

Note: Construction work means any construction, alteration, and/or repair, including painting and decorating. The asterisks indicate activities that may, under some circumstances, fall under the general industry lead standard 29 CFR 1910.1025.

Every observation of any operation where there exists the potential for lead exposure will be handled as follows:

- Whenever an inspector observes or receives information, regardless of whether or not a violation is observed, through nonformal complaints, referrals, reports from members of the general public, and so forth, the inspector will:

  - Document the status and condition of the work operation as far as it is known, noting any serious hazards.

  - Note the name and address and location of the worksite and the contractor(s) performing the operation.

  - Provide the area office supervisor or area director with the information. Based upon the information provided, all potential lead in construction work sites brought to the attention of the area office shall be investigated/inspected as follows:

    - If the worksite has been inspected within the last 30 days, the results of the inspection shall be considered along with the current worksite observations in determining whether or not an inspection is to be conducted.

    - If the lead-related work was not in progress during the previous visit to the site but is currently in progress the inspection shall be authorized and opened.

    - If the lead-related work was in progress and evaluated during the previous inspection, the inspection will be opened only if apparent serious violations are present or can reasonably be expected at the site.

Special Emphasis and Focused Programs

- If the worksite has not been inspected within the previous 30 days, an investigation/inspection shall be conducted unless it is apparent that workers are not exposed to lead.

- Reports of imminent danger, fatality/catastrophe reports, formal/nonformal complaints, safety and health referrals from other federal, state, county, and city agencies, media reports, reports for physicians, hospitals, or medical clinics, and reports from the general public shall be investigated/inspected by the area office.

- The discovery of these work sites may be the result of a specific search to find this type of operation, at the discretion of the regional administrator. Although sightings will be those normally that occur during the course of routine travel during duty or non-duty hours, regional policy may provide that the area director saturate areas of high construction activity to identify potential lead in construction work sites.

Documentation of the events leading up to the observation shall be maintained by the area office in case of a denial of entry.

Area offices

OSHA area offices will be encouraged to develop a list of construction contractors under their jurisdiction likely to be involved in lead related activities. SIC Codes most likely to be included in the list involve 1622 (bridge tunnel, and elevated highway construction), 1629 (heavy construction), 1721 (painting and paperhanging), 1791 (structural steel erection), 1795 (wrecking and demolition work), and 1799 (special trade contractors not elsewhere classified).

Application

Inspections under this SEP will address all aspects of any potential lead work or exposure and include a review of all related written documentation (i.e., record keeping, monitoring, medical, respirator fit testing and procedures, hazard communication, and training materials). The inspector may expand the inspection scope beyond the lead related activities if hazards or violations are observed.

Inspectors will conduct personal monitoring and collect wipe samples as appropriate to document exposures.

While evaluating worker exposures to lead, inspectors will also need to be aware of and evaluate potential exposures to other metals including but not limited to arsenic, manganese, chromium, cadmium, copper, and magnesium.

Trenching and Excavations—OSHA's Special Emphasis Program

OSHA's CPL 2.69 establishes a National Emphasis Program for the programmed safety inspection of trenching and excavation operations.

Background

Because of the continuing incidence of trench/excavation collapses and accompanying loss of life, OSHA has determined that an increased enforcement presence at worksites where such operations are being conducted is warranted.

Trenching and excavation work creates hazards to workers which are extremely dangerous. Compliance with OSHA construction standards applicable to such operations is frequently bypassed because of economic pressures, a belief that compliance is unnecessary, or an expectation that these short-term operations will go undetected.

Although it would be expected that, after more than 12 years of enforcement activity, most employers would be adhering to shoring and sloping requirements, experience has shown that such is not the case.

OSHA believes that the rate of deaths and serious injuries resulting from trench/excavation accidents (mostly cave-ins) can be significantly affected only by a concentration of compliance resources within the area of trenching and excavation operations.

Currently six of OSHA's ten regions are already conducting local emphasis programs in this area. These local emphasis programs are all similar in nature. The decision has been made to replace these programs with a National Emphasis Program extended to all regions.

Procedures

All OSHA inspectors are instructed to be on the lookout for trenching or excavation worksites. Every observation of such operations will be handled as follows:

- Regardless of whether or not a violation is observed, whenever an inspector sights or receives any other notice of a trenching or excavation operation (including nonformal complaints, other government agency referrals, and reports from members of the public) the inspector will:

    - Make note of the state and condition of the work operation insofar as it is known, including any apparent serious hazards.

    - Note the name and address or location of the worksite and the contractor performing the operation, if known.

    - Contact the area office supervisor for a decision as to whether an inspection is required.

Special Emphasis and Focused Programs

- All trenching and excavation worksites brought to the attention of the area office will be inspected as follows:
    - If the worksite has been inspected within the last 30 days, the results of the inspection shall be considered along with the current observations of the inspector.
        - If trenching/excavation work was not in progress during the last inspection and there are apparent serious violations present at the current site, the supervisor shall authorize an inspection.
        - If trenching/excavation work was in progress during the last inspection, the supervisor shall authorize an inspection only if apparent serious violations are present or can reasonably be expected at the current site.
    - If the worksite has not been inspected within the last 30 days, an inspection shall be conducted unless it is apparent that the trench or excavation is less than 5 feet deep or is in compliance with all OSHA standards governing such operations.

The discovery of these worksites may be the result of a specific search to find this type of operation, at the discretion of the regional administrator. Although sightings normally will be those which occur during the course of routine travel during duty or nonduty hours, regional policy may provide that the area director saturate areas of high construction activity for the purpose of identifying all trenching and excavation sites within that area as far as reasonably possible.

Documentation of the events leading up to the observation or the reporting of the trenching or excavation worksite will be maintained by the area office in case of denial of entry.

When an inspection is not conducted because consent has not been obtained, a warrant normally will be sought in accordance with the current procedure for handling such cases. A warrant may not be necessary, however, if the violations are in plain view. In such situations, the regional administrator will contact the regional solicitor for guidance.

If the inspector initially observing the work operation involving a trenching or excavation operation sees an apparently serious hazard in plain view, and if it is not convenient to contact the supervisor at the time, an inspection will be conducted and the supervisor informed as soon as practical after the inspection has been completed.

When conducting inspections in trenching or excavation operations, inspectors will be alert to the presence of minors who may be employed at a worksite. Because the Employment Standards Administration (ESA) has regulations related to the employment of minors between 16 and 18 years old in hazardous occupations, any indication during a trenching or excavation inspection that minors are so employed will be reported as soon as reasonably possible to the area director who will relay this information to the nearest wage-hour area office immediately. The regional administrator will be informed whenever such a referral has been made.

OSHA's Focused Inspection Initiative for Construction Jobsites

On October 1, 1994, OSHA kicked off its Focused Inspections Initiative for construction sites. This program deviates quite radically from OSHA's old way of doing business; it recognizes the efforts of responsible contractors who have implemented effective safety and health programs/plans. It also encourages other contractors to adopt similar programs.

The "number of inspections" is no longer driving the construction inspection program according to a "Memorandum to Regional Administrators" from James W. Stanley, Deputy Assistant Secretary, dated August 22, 1994 and revised September 20, 1995.

Under previous OSHA policy, all construction inspections were in-depth and addressed all areas and all classes of hazards at a worksite. This policy may have caused compliance officers to spend too much time and effort on a few projects looking for all violations when they could have inspected many projects looking for hazards which are most likely to cause fatalities and serious injuries to workers.

Previously, you were likely to be cited for hazards that were unrelated to the four leading causes of death: falls from elevation, struck by, caught in/between, and electrical hazards. These make up 90% of all construction fatalities.

All unsafe conditions are important. However, the time and resources spent to pursue them on a few projects can be better spent pursuing conditions on many projects related to the four hazard areas most likely to cause serious injuries or fatalities. The goal of OSHA's construction inspections is to make a difference in the safety and health of employees at the worksite. To accomplish this, the OSHA inspector's time will be more effectively spent inspecting the most hazardous workplace conditions. The inspectors will conduct comprehensive, resource intensive, inspections only on those projects where there is inadequate contractor commitment to safety and health. It is this group of employers that will receive OSHA's full attention.

What kind of inspection will you get?

Some of the rules of the focused inspection are new and some are old. When an inspector shows up at your company for a normal programmed inspection the opening conference will be as it is now, with the inspector determining whether or not there is:

- Project coordination by the general contractor, prime contractor, or other such entity.

- An adequate safety and health program/plan that meets the requirements of 29 CFR 1926 Subpart C—General safety and health provisions, and other OSHA guidelines (see guidelines next section).

- A designated competent person, responsible for, and capable of implementing the program/plan.

Special Emphasis and Focused Programs

If these criteria are met, then an abbreviated walkaround inspection will be made. When these criteria are not met, then the inspection will proceed in accordance with previously established procedures for comprehensive inspections as stated in OSHA's Field Inspection Reference Manual (FIRM).

If the inspection is a fatality/catastrophe complaint, or referral inspection, the inspector will inspect the worksite in regard to the fatality/complaint/referral items and then can proceed to a focused inspection scenario.

At some time during an inspection, you and your employee representative should be informed why a focused or a comprehensive inspection is being conducted. This can be accomplished by the inspector verbally or by posting the "Handout for Contractors and Employees." A copy of this handout is on page 87.

What criteria will likely be used to evaluate your safety and health program/plan?

The guidelines an OSHA inspector will use to evaluate your safety and health program will include:

- The comprehensiveness of your program/plan. Examples of good, comprehensive, safety and health programs can be found in:
  - The Safety and Health Program Management Guidelines published in the *Federal Register* January 26, 1989.
  - The ANSI A10.33 *Safety and Health Program Requirements for Multi-Employer Projects.*
  - Owner and Contractor Association model programs that meet the 29 CFR 1926 Subpart C standards.
- The degree of program/plan implementation.
- The designation of competent persons as required by relevant standards.
- How your program/plan is enforced including management policies and activities, effective employee involvement, and training. Employees will be interviewed during the walk around to aid in the evaluation of the program/plan.

A brief justification as to why a focused inspection was or was not conducted will be included in your case file. The optional "Construction Focused Inspection Guideline" can be used by the inspector for this purpose. A copy of this inspector guideline is on page 88.

What will focused inspections concentrate on?

Focused inspections will concentrate on your project safety and health program/plan and the four leading hazards that account for the most fatalities and serious injuries in the construction industry: falls, electrical hazards, caught in/between hazards, and struck by hazards.

During focused inspections, citations will be proposed for violations of these four leading hazards and any other serious hazards observed.

Other-than-serious hazards that are abated immediately, and this abatement is observed by the inspecting officer, will not normally be cited nor documented.

If during the walkaround the inspector determines that the number of serious and other-than-serious hazards found on the project indicate that the safety and health program/plan is inadequate or is ineffectively implemented, then the inspection will be comprehensive. The discovery of serious violations need not automatically convert the focused inspection into a comprehensive inspection. These decisions will be based on the professional judgement of the inspecting officer.

Only contractors on projects that qualify for a focused inspection will be eligible to receive a full "good faith" adjustment of 25% for citations.

Resources to help you with your worksite program/plan

The sources you can use to prepare for an OSHA focused inspection are the same ones the inspector will be using. These are listed on the previous page. In addition, you can use ANSI A10.38—*Basic Elements of an Employer Program to Provide a Safe and Healthful Work Environment* to help in your preparation. And as always you need a copy of the Safety and Health Regulations for Construction found at 29 CFR 1926, Subpart C.

Special Emphasis and Focused Programs

CONSTRUCTION FOCUSED INSPECTIONS INITIATIVE

Handout for Contractors and Employees

The goal of Focused Inspections is to reduce injuries, illness and fatalities by concentrating OSHA enforcement on those projects that do not have effective safety and health programs/plans and limiting OSHA's time spent on projects with effective programs/plans.

To qualify for a Focused Inspection the project safety and health program/plan will be reviewed and a walkaround will be made of the jobsite to verify that the program/plan is being fully implemented.

During the walkaround the compliance officer will focus on the four leading hazards that cause 90% of deaths and injuries in construction. The leading hazards are:

- Falls (e.g., floors, platforms, roofs).
- Struck by (e.g., falling objects, vehicles).
- Caught in/between (e.g., cave-ins, unguarded machinery, equipment).
- Electrical (e.g., overhead power lines, power tools and cords, outlets, temporary wiring).

The compliance officer will interview employees to determine their knowledge of the safety and health program/plan, their awareness of potential jobsite hazards, their training in hazard recognition, and their understanding of applicable OSHA standards.

If the project safety and health program/plan is found to be effectively implemented the compliance officer will terminate the inspection.

If the project does not qualify for a Focused Inspection, the compliance officer will conduct a comprehensive inspection of the entire project.

If you have any questions or concerns related to the inspection or conditions on the project, you are encouraged to bring them to the immediate attention of the compliance officer or call the area office at:

_____.

_____ **qualified as a FOCUSED PROJECT.**
(Project/Site)

_____   _____.
(Date)   (AREA DIRECTOR)

This document should be distributed at the site and given to the Contractor for posting.

CONSTRUCTION FOCUSED INSPECTION GUIDELINE

This guideline is to assist the professional judgement of the compliance officer to determine if there is an effective project plan, to qualify for a Focused Inspection.

	YES/NO
PROJECT SAFETY AND HEALTH COORDINATION: are there procedures in place by the general contractor, prime contractor or other such entity to ensure that all employers provide adequate protection for their employees?	
Is there a DESIGNATED COMPETENT PERSON responsible for the implementation and monitoring of the project safety and health plan who is capable of identifying existing and predictable hazards and has authority to take prompt corrective measures?	
Is there a PROJECT SAFETY AND HEALTH PROGRAM/PLAN* that complies with 1926 Subpart C and addresses, based upon the size and complexity of the project, the following:	

_____   Project Safety Analysis at initiation and at critical stages that describes the sequence, procedures, and responsible individuals for safe construction.

_____   Identification of work/activities requiring planning, design, inspection or supervision by an engineer, competent person or other professional.

_____   Evaluation/monitoring of subcontractors to determine conformance with the Project Plan. (The Project Plan may include, or be utilized by subcontractors.)

_____   Supervisor and employee training according to the Project Plan including recognition, reporting and avoidance of hazards, and applicable standards.

_____   Procedures for controlling hazardous operations such as: cranes, scaffolding, trenches, confined spaces, hot work, explosives, hazardous materials, leading edges, etc.

_____   Documentation of: training, permits, hazard reports, inspections, uncorrected hazards, incidents and near misses.

_____   Employee involvement in hazard: analysis, prevention, avoidance, correction and reporting.

_____   Project emergency response plan.

* FOR EXAMPLES, SEE OWNER AND CONTRACTOR ASSOCIATION MODEL PROGRAMS, ANSI A10.33, A10.38, ETC.

The walkaround and interviews confirmed that the Plan has been implemented, including:

_____   The four leading hazards are addressed: falls, struck by, caught in/between, electrical.

_____   Hazards are identified and corrected with preventative measures instituted in a timely manner.

_____   Employees and supervisors are knowledgeable of the project safety and health plan, avoidance of hazards, applicable standards, and their rights and responsibilities.

THE PROJECT QUALIFIED FOR A FOCUSED INSPECTION

Other OSHA Special Interest Areas

Residential Construction—OSHA's Interim Fall Protection Compliance Guidelines

Purpose

Fall protection requirements for residential construction are in 29 CFR 1926.501(b)(13). In general, that provision requires conventional fall protection for work at or over six feet. However, OSHA Instruction STD 3.1A modifies those requirements. It permits employers engaged in certain residential construction activities to use alternative procedures routinely instead of conventional fall protection. No showing of infeasibility of conventional fall protection is needed before using these procedures. A fall protection plan is required but it does not have to be written nor does it have to be specific to the jobsite. Different alternative procedures are specified for different activities.

Availability of alternative procedures

These alternative procedures are available to employers who are: (1) engaged in residential construction, and (2) doing one of the listed activities.

An employer is engaged in residential construction where the working environment, materials, methods and procedures are essentially the same as those used in building a typical single-family home or townhouse.

Residential construction is characterized by:

- Materials: Wood framing (not steel or concrete); wooden floor joists and roof structures.
- Methods: Traditional wood frame construction techniques.

In addition, the construction of a discrete part of a large commercial building (not the entire building), such as a wood frame shingled entranceway to a mall, may fit within the definition of residential construction. Such discrete parts of a commercial building would qualify as residential construction where the characteristics listed above are present.

Listed activities and alternative procedures

There are four groups of residential construction activities for which alternative fall protection plans are available. Each group has its own set of alternative procedures.

The groups are:

Group 1—Installation of floor joists, floor and roof sheathing, erecting exterior walls, setting and bracing roof trusses and rafters.

Group 2—Working on concrete and block foundation walls and related formwork.

Group 3—This group consists of the following activities when performed in attics and on roofs: installing drywall, insulation, HVAC systems, electrical systems (including alarms, telephone lines, and cable TV), plumbing, and carpentry.

Group 4—Roofing work (removal, repair, or installation of weatherproofing roofing materials such as shingles, tile and tar paper).

Questions

Do any of these plans have to be written and site specific? No.

Does the employer have to determine that conventional fall protection is infeasible before being permitted to use an alternative procedure? No.

Alternative procedures for Groups 1 - 4

The alternative measures for groups 1-4 are quite lengthy and not suitable for the intended format of this manual. If you are engaged in certain residential construction and are interested in using alternative procedures routinely instead of conventional fall protection, you should obtain a copy of OSHA's STD 3-0.1A—*Plain Language Revision of OSHA Instruction 3.1, Interim Fall Protection Compliance Guidelines for Residential Construction* for the alternative procedures for Groups 1-4.

Citation policy

If an employer (engaged in residential construction) does not provide conventional fall protection, the inspector must determine if STD 3-0.1A provides alternative procedures for the activity in question. If alternative procedures are available, the inspector must determine if they have been implemented. If there is a deficiency in the implementation of the alternative procedures, the fall hazard shall be cited as a violation of 29 CFR 1926.501(b)(13). No other provision may be cited for a fall hazard addressed by 1926.501(b)(13).

Deficiencies in training required by 1926.20 may also be cited where appropriate.

Other Special Interest Areas

Steel Erection—OSHA's Interim Fall Protection Compliance Guidelines

The Occupational Safety and Health Administration (OSHA) has published a compliance directive 00-03 (CPL 2-1) to describe their enforcement policy for steel erection in the interim period between the publication of the proposed rule and enactment of the final rule.

The compliance directive:

- Supercedes and cancels OSHA's July 10, 1995 *Interim fall protection enforcement policy for steel erectors* memorandum to regional administrators.

- Extends the policies and procedures of OSHA Notice 99-1 (CPL 2-1) for another year but may be renewed.

- Requires OSHA regional and area directors to ensure their inspectors are familiar with the directive and that the enforcement guidelines are followed.

- Expires on February 10, 2001.

Background

In August 1998, OSHA published a proposed rule for steel erection. This current CPL describes OSHA's enforcement policy for steel erection in this interim period between the publication of the proposed rule and enactment of a final rule.

OSHA's Field Inspection Reference Manual (FIRM) states that compliance with a proposed standard, rather than with the standard in effect, would be considered a De Minimis violation provided that the employer's action clearly provides equal or greater employee protection. De Minimis violations are not cited.

In accordance with the FIRM, OSHA establishes the following steel erection enforcement policy:

Options

Until the release of the final steel erection rule, employers engaged in steel erection must follow either:

- The current steel erection rules (29 CFR 1926.750-.752 and 1926.105(a)), or

- The proposed steel erection regulation published in the *Federal Register* on August 13, 1998, with one exception. The proposed rule allows deckers (working in a controlled decking zone) to work up to 30 feet before fall protection is required. The current standard (1926.105(a)) requires deckers working in single tiered buildings to be protected from falls at 25 feet. The current 25 foot requirement will continue to be enforced.

Scope and application to be followed for compliance with current rules

The scope of steel erection activities in the current rules differs somewhat from the scope of the proposed rule.

NOTE: Paragraphs 29 CFR 1926.104, 1926.105, and 1926.107(b), (c), and (f) apply to steel erection activities.

Steel erection activities include:

The movement and erection of skeleton steel members (structural steel), including initial connecting, moving point-to-point, installing metal floor or roof decking, welding, bolting, and similar activities. Steel erection also includes these activities when structural steel is installed on concrete and masonry walls or supports.

Activities that are not steel erection:

Steel erection does not include the erection of steel members such as lintels, stairs, railings, curtainwalls, windows, architectural metalwork, column covers, catwalks, and similar non-skeletal items, nor does it mean the placement of reinforcing rods in concrete structures.

NOTE: These steel erection activities may take place in buildings and other structures. *Buildings* include tiered and non-tiered, single-story and multi-story buildings, warehouses, gymnasiums, stadiums, power plants, theaters, mill buildings, and similar structures. *Tiered* means the skeleton steel framework is erected in vertically stacked columns; tiered structures are not limited to multi-floored structures. *Other structures* include bridges, viaducts, overpasses, towers, tanks, billboards, antennas, and similar structures.

Application of fall protection requirements

Tiered buildings

- Exterior fall hazards of 25 feet or more are covered by 1926.105(a). Fall protection is not required for exterior fall hazards of less than 25 feet.

- Interior fall hazards of 30 feet or more on buildings which have floors or are adaptable to temporary floors are covered by 1926.750(b)(2)(i). Fall protection is not required for fall hazards of less than 30 feet. Temporary floors will generally be practicable in the construction of a typical multi-floored building.

- Interior fall hazards of 25 feet or more on tiered buildings which are not adaptable to temporary floors are covered by 1926.750(b)(1)(ii). Fall protection is not required for fall hazards of less than 25 feet.

Non-tiered buildings

Exterior and interior fall hazards of 25 feet or more are covered by 1926.105(a). Fall protection is not required for fall hazards of less than 25 feet.

Other Special Interest Areas

Other structures

Exterior and interior fall hazards of 25 feet or more are covered by 1926.105(a). Fall protection is not required for fall hazards of less than 25 feet.

Scope and application to be followed for compliance with the proposed rule

The activities and structures covered by the proposed rule are quite lengthy. If you want to use the proposed steel erection rule as your guide for steel erection activities, you should obtain a copy of the proposed rule and the compliance directive CPL 2-1—Steel Erection

Communication Tower Construction Activities—Interim Inspection Procedures

OSHA's CPL 2-1.29 describes OSHA's inspection policy and procedures to ensure uniform enforcement by OSHA inspectors of the provisions addressing fall protection and safe access to communications towers during construction.

Application

This instruction applies only to the construction of new communications towers. Activities such as maintenance, retrofitting, and dismantling will be addressed in a future directive.

Background

Accessing towers using fixed ladders with attached climbing devices has been the preferred method as it provides conventional fall protection during ascent and descent of the structure. Some representatives of the tower construction industry assert that continual climbing of high towers is physically demanding and can lead to stress and medical ailments over an extended period of time and may contribute to other safety problems including falls. To alleviate these problems, the industry has asked that employees be allowed to ride a hoist line to work stations on towers. Since OSHA does not specifically address tower erection under its current standards but wishes to help reduce the accident and injury rates associated with tower erection, OSHA believes that the methods in Appendix A represent the best practices which can be implemented to safeguard employees while being hoisted to work stations on the tower. If new information shows that these practices need to be changed, OSHA will revise this directive accordingly.

Compliance guidelines

For purposes of this directive, OSHA agrees that the hoist line may be used to hoist employees for access to tower work stations over 200 feet high if the work practices and requirements set out in Appendix A are followed. At heights of 200 feet and below, employees may not be hoisted to their work stations using the hoist line.

When climbing the tower during construction activities, employees must be protected from falls using a fall arrest system meeting the criteria of §1926.502 or a ladder assist safety device meeting the requirements of §1926.1053(a). These are acceptable methods of accessing tower work stations regardless of height. All employees climbing or otherwise accessing towers must be trained in the recognition and avoidance of fall hazards and in the use of the fall protection systems to be used, pursuant to §1926.21 or where applicable, §1926.1060.

Some industry representatives have joined with OSHA in recommending that each employee six feet or more above a lower level should be protected from falling by a guardrail system, safety net system, ladder safety device, fall arrest system, or positioning device system. However, current OSHA standards only require fall protection at heights of more than 25 feet.

Citation guidelines

For hazards associated with falls once employees are at their workstation at levels in excess of 25 feet, employers who fail to provide fall protection will be cited under §1926.105(a).

Whenever an employer fails to follow the guidelines set forth in Appendix A, citations will be issued under the applicable provisions of subpart N and, in the alternative, section 5(a)(1) of the OSH Act (the general duty clause) for hazards associated with work practices and equipment used to hoist employees on load lines to gain access to towers.

Appendix A

Definitions

Crew chief—One who is authorized, designated, deemed competent, and qualified by the employer.

Anti-two blocking—A positive acting device which prevents contact between the load block or overhaul ball and the top block (two-blocking), or a system which deactivates the hoisting action before damage occurs in the event of a two-block situation.

Maximum intended load—The total load of all employees, tools, materials, load lines, and other loads reasonably anticipated to be applied to the hoist apparatus when an employee is hoisted.

Competent person—One who is capable of identifying existing and predictable hazards in the surroundings or working conditions which are unsanitary, hazardous, or dangerous to employees and who has authorization to take prompt corrective measures to eliminate problems.

Authorized person—A person approved or assigned by the employer to perform a specific type of duty or duties or to be at a specific location or locations at the job site.

Qualified—One who, by possession of a recognized degree, certificate, or professional standing, or who by extensive knowledge, training, and experience, has successfully demonstrated the ability to solve or resolve problems relating to the subject matter, the work, or the project.

Other Special Interest Areas

Gin pole—A device attached to the tower used to raise sections of tower steel or equipment into position.

Specific requirements

Employees may be hoisted on the hoist line to reach work stations at heights greater than 200 feet only if all of the following conditions are met. OSHA believes that strict adherence to the guidelines set forth in this Appendix will provide employers with the appropriate safety measures for access during tower erection. Riding the hoist line to work stations at heights less than 200 feet is not permitted.

Training

Before an employee is allowed to perform any job related to hoisting employees aloft for tower work, the employee must receive training on safe access pursuant to these guidelines. The operator of the hoist must have a thorough understanding of these guidelines pertaining to hoisting employees on the hoist line.

Equipment

An anti-two block device must be used on all hoists, except where an employer can demonstrate that ambient radiation frequency (RF) precludes that use. In such case, a site specific program will be established and maintained on site to ensure that two blocking cannot occur and that effective communication between the hoist operator and personnel being hoisted is maintained. This program could include a cable marking system, an employee situated on the tower in a position to observe the top block, or any other system which will adequately ensure communication.

The rigging, hoist line, and slings must have a factor of safety of 10 against failure during personnel lift(s).

The hoist line used to raise or lower employees must be equipped with a swivel to prevent any rotation of the employees.

The use of spin-resistant wire rope is prohibited when hoisting employees.

When hoisting personnel (versus material) the hoist capacity load rating must be derated by a factor of 2 (reduced by half).

All employees must be provided with and required to use the proper personal protective equipment (including fall protection equipment) which must be inspected before each lift.

Except where the employer can demonstrate that specific circumstances or conditions preclude its use, a guide line (tag line) must be used to prevent the employees or the platform from contacting the tower during hoisting.

The gin pole must be thoroughly inspected before use by a competent person to determine that it is free from defects, including but not limited to: damaged and/or missing members; corrosive damage; missing fasteners and broken welds at joints; and general deterioration.

The gin pole must be attached to the tower as designed by a registered professional engineer. There must be a minimum of two attachment locations: at the bottom of the gin pole, and near the top of the tower being erected.

The personnel load capacity and material capacity of the lifting system in use must be posted at the site near the location of the hoist operator. If the system is changed (for example, if the gin pole angle is changed), the posted capacity must be changed accordingly.

Trial lift and proof testing

A trial lift of the maximum intended personnel load must be made from ground level to the location to which personnel are to be hoisted.

The trial lift must be made immediately prior to placing personnel on the hoist line. The hoist operator must determine that all systems, controls, and safety devices are activated and functioning properly. A single trial lift may be performed for all locations that are to be reached from a single set-up position. The hoist operator must determine that no interference exists and that all configurations necessary to reach those work locations remain under the limit of the hoist's rated capacity as identified in the previous section (equipment), and additionally maintain a 10:1 factor of safety against failure.

The trial lift must be repeated prior to hoisting employees whenever the hoist is moved and set up in a new location or returned to a previously used position.

After the trial lift, employees must not be lifted unless the following conditions are met:

- Hoist wire ropes are determined to be free of damage in accordance with the provisions of §1926.550.

- Multiple part lines are not twisted around each other.

- The proof testing requirements have been satisfied.

If the hoist wire rope is slack, the hoisting system must be inspected to ensure that all wire ropes are properly seated on drums and in sheaves.

A visual inspection of the hoist, rigging, base support, and foundation must be made by a competent person immediately after the trial lift to determine whether testing has exposed any defect or adverse effect upon any component of the structure.

Any defects found during the inspection which may create a safety hazard must be corrected, and another trial lift must be performed before hoisting personnel.

Prior to hoisting employees and after any repair or modification, the personnel rigging must be proof tested to 125% of the greatest anticipated load by holding it in a suspended position for five minutes with the test load evenly distributed (this may be done concurrently with the

Other Special Interest Areas

trial lift). After proof testing, a competent person must inspect the rigging. Any deficiencies found must be corrected and another proof test must be conducted.

Pre-lift meeting

A pre-lift meeting must be held prior to the trial lift at each location.

The pre-lift meeting must:

- Be attended by the hoist operator, employees to be lifted, and the crew chief.
- Review the procedures to be followed and all appropriate requirements contained in this guideline.
- Be repeated for any employee newly assigned to the operation.

Documentation

All trial lifts, inspections, and proof tests must be documented, and the documentation must remain on site during the entire length of the project.

The pre-lift meeting must be documented, and the documentation must remain on site during the entire length of the project.

Hoisting an employee to the work station

Except where an employer can demonstrate that specific circumstances or conditions preclude its use, a personnel platform must be used to hoist more than one employee to the work station. That personnel platform must meet the requirements of §1926.550(g). When a personnel platform cannot be used, the following provisions must be followed.

When a boatswains seat-type or full body seat harness is used to hoist employees, the following must apply:

- No more than two employees may be hoisted at a time.
- The employee's harness must be attached to the hook by a lanyard meeting the strength requirements of §1926.502.
- Only locking-type snap hooks must be used.
- The harness must be equipped with two side rings and at least one front and one back D ring.

The hoist line hook must be equipped with a safety latch which can be locked in a closed position to prevent loss of contact.

The maximum rate of travel must not exceed 200 feet per minute when a guide line is used to control personnel hoists. When a guide line cannot be used, the rate of travel of the employee being hoisted must not exceed 100 feet per minute. In all personnel hoist situations, the maximum rate must not exceed 50 feet per minute when personnel being lifted approach to within 50 feet of the top block.

The use of free-spooling (friction lowering) is prohibited.

When the hoist line is being used to raise or lower employee(s), there must be no other load attached to any hoist line, and no other load must be raised or lowered at the same time on the same hoist.

As-built drawings approved by a registered professional engineer must provide the lifting capacity of the gin pole and must be available at the job site.

The gin pole raising line must not be used to raise or lower employees.

Employees must maintain 100% tie-off while moving between the hoist line and the tower.

Communication between the hoist operator and hoisted employees

Employees being hoisted must remain in continuous sight of and/or in direct communication with the operator or signal person. In those situations where direct visual contact with the operator is not possible and the use of a signal person would create a greater hazard for the person being hoisted, direct communication alone, such as by radio, must be used.

When radios are used, they must be non-trunking closed 2-way selective frequency systems.

When hand signals are used, the employees must use industry standardized hand signals as required by §1926.550(a)(4).

Weather conditions/Energized power lines

Employees must not be hoisted during adverse weather conditions (high winds, electrical storms, snow, ice, sleet), or other impending danger, except in the case of emergency employee rescue. This determination must be made by the competent person.

The hoist system (gin pole and its base hoists) used to raise and lower employees on the hoist line, must not be used unless the following clearance distances as recommended by ANSI are maintained at all times during the lift:

Power line voltage phase to phase (kV)	Minimum safe clearance (feet)
50 or below	10
Above 50 to 200	15
Above 200 to 350	20
Above 350 to 500	25
Above 500 to 750	35
Above 750 to 1,000	45

Other Special Interest Areas

Hydraulic hoists (drum hoists)

The hoist used for personnel lifting must meet the applicable requirements for design, construction, installation, testing, inspection, maintenance, modification, repair and operations as referenced in this Appendix and as prescribed by the manufacturer. Where manufacturers' specifications are not available, the limitations assigned to the equipment must be based on the determinations of a registered professional engineer.

The hoist must be positioned so that it is level and the distance between the drum and the foot block at the base of the tower will allow proper spooling of wire rope.

The foot block must be anchored to prevent displacement and be supported to maintain proper alignment.

The hoist must be designed to lift materials and personnel with the same drum or drums.

Any hoist that has been modified or repaired must be proof-tested to 125% of its rated capacity.

Rated load capacities, recommended operating speeds, and special hazard warnings or instructions, must be conspicuously posted on all hoists.

Belts, gears, shafts, pulleys, sprockets, spindles, drums, fly wheels, chains, or other rotating parts, where exposed, must be totally enclosed.

Personnel load capacity for the current configuration of the gin pole must be posted within sight of the hoist operator.

The hoist must have an hour meter and a line speed limiter.

The hoist must be designed for and must use powered lowering.

The alignment of hoist components must be maintained within manufacturer's specified limits that prevent premature deterioration of gear teeth, bearings, splines, bushings, and any other parts of the hoist mechanism.

All exhaust pipes must be guarded where exposed.

An accessible fire extinguisher of 5BC rating or higher must be available at the operator's station.

The hoist must be serviced and maintained per the manufacturer's recommendations.

The operating manual developed by the manufacturer for the specific make and model hoist being used must be maintained at the site at all times.

A hoist log book must be used to record all hoist inspections, tests, maintenance, and repair. The log must be updated daily as the hoist is being used and must be signed by the operator and/or crew chief. Service mechanics must sign the log after conducting maintenance and repair. The log must be maintained at the site.

Hoist mounting

The hoist must be installed following the manufacturer's mounting procedure to prevent excessive distortion of the hoist base as it is attached to the mounting surface. Flatness of the mounting surface must be held to tolerances specified by the hoist manufacturer.

The hoist must be anchored so as to resist at least two times any reaction induced at the maximum attainable line pull and must be anchored so that the hoist will not twist or turn.

If the hoist is mounted to a truck chassis, it must be properly aligned and anchored in at least two corners to prevent movement, and the wheels must be properly chocked.

Drums

The hoist drum must be capable of raising or lowering 125% of the rated load of the hoist.

The hoist drum must have a positive means of attaching the wire rope to the drum.

There must always be at least three full wraps of wire rope on the hoist drum when personnel are being hoisted.

During operation, the flange must be two times the wire rope diameter higher than the top layer of wire rope at all times.

Brakes and clutches

Brakes and clutches must be capable of arresting any over-speed descent of the load.

The hoist must be provided with a primary brake and at least one independent secondary brake, each capable of stopping and holding 125% of the lifting capacity of the hoist.

The primary brake must be directly connected to the drive train of the hoisting machine, and must not be connected through belts, chains, clutches, or screw-type devices.

The secondary brake must be an automatic emergency-type brake that, if actuated during each stopping cycle, must not engage before the hoist is stopped by the primary brake.

When a secondary brake is actuated, it must stop and hold the load within a vertical distance of 24 inches.

Brakes and clutches must be adjusted, where necessary, to compensate for wear and to maintain adequate force on springs where used.

Powered lowering must be used.

When power brakes having no continuous mechanical linkage between the actuating and braking mechanism are used for controlling loads, an automatic means must be provided to set the brake to prevent the load from falling in the event of loss of brake actuating power.

Static brakes must be provided to prevent the drum from rotating in the lowering direction and must be capable of holding the rated load indefinitely without attention from the operator.

Other Special Interest Areas

Brakes must be automatically applied upon return of the control lever to its center (neutral) position.

Brakes applied on stopped hoist drums must have sufficient impact capacity to hold 1.5 times the rated torque of the hoist.

Hoist controls

Power plant controls must be within easy reach of the operator and must include a means to start and stop, control speed of internal combustion engines, stop prime mover under emergency conditions, and shift selective transmissions.

All controls used during the normal operation of the hoist must be located within easy reach of the operator at the operator's station.

Controls must be clearly marked (or be part of a control arrangement diagram) and easily visible from the operator's station.

Foot-operated pedals, where provided, must be constructed and maintained so the operator's feet will not readily slip off and the force necessary to move the pedals can be easily applied.

The controls must be self-centering controls (i.e., "deadman" type) that will return the machine to neutral and engage the drum brakes if the control lever is released.

Wire rope and rigging

All wire rope and rigging must be inspected daily before use.

All eyes in wire rope slings must be fabricated with thimbles.

All eyes in wire rope slings must:

- Be made with swaged-type fittings.
- Be field fabricated by a qualified person or factory made.

Hoist operator

The hoist operator must have classroom training, a minimum of 40 hours experience as a hoist operator, not less than 8 hours experience in the operation of the specified hoist or one of the same type, and demonstrated the ability to safely operate the hoist.

The employer must not allow an employee to operate a hoist when that employee is physically or mentally unfit.

The hoist operator must be responsible for those operations under his/her direct control. Whenever there is any doubt as to safety, the operator must have the authority to stop and refuse to handle the load until safety has been assured.

The hoist operator must remain at the controls at all times when personnel are on the hoist line.

Before starting the hoist, the operator must ensure that:

- The daily inspection has been conducted.
- All controls are in the "off" position.
- All personnel are in the clear.

Hoist inspections

Routine inspections

Each day before use all hoists must be visually inspected by a qualified person.

All hoists must be inspected thoroughly at three month intervals by a qualified person, as will any hoists that have been idle for more than one month but less than six months. Such inspection will include a hands-on operation of all moving parts to ensure that they are intact and will properly function before being put into service.

Tear-down inspections

All hoists must undergo a tear-down inspection annually unless the following conditions exist that allow for less frequent tear-down inspections.

A hoist that has been idle for a period of over six (6) months must be given an annual inspection which includes the hoist being completely disassembled, cleaned and inspected. Parts such as pins, bearings, shafts, gears, brake plates, etc. found worn, cracked, corroded, distorted or otherwise non-functional must be replaced before the hoist is used.

Hoists with infrequent to moderate usage (hoists that have been used for fifty (50) hours or less per month and normally operate at considerably less than the hoist rated capacity based on the average use over a month) may go up to thirty-six (36) months between tear down inspections if serviced under a preventive maintenance program (as specified by the manufacturer) that includes annual hydraulic oil sample analysis. An oil sample analysis, meaning a laboratory analysis, is used to evaluate the mechanical integrity of the hoist. Oil in these hoists must be changed at least annually, just after the oil analysis is performed. Hoists not subjected to recommended oil sample analysis must undergo an annual tear-down inspection.

Hoists that experience heavy usage (hoists that are used for more than fifty (50) hours per month) may go up to twenty-four (24) months between tear-down inspections if serviced under a preventive maintenance program as in the paragraph above.

Any rebuilt hoist assembly must be line pull tested to the rated load. The hoist drum must be rotated several times in both raising and lowering directions under full-rated load, while checking for smooth operation.

Other Special Interest Areas

Work Zone Safety

What is a work zone?

A work zone is an area where roadwork is going on and traffic is affected. Construction or utility work done outside the roadway is not considered work zone activity. Examples of work zone activity include: building a new bridge; adding travel lanes to the roadway; extending an existing roadway; repairing potholes; and repairing electric, gas, or water lines within the roadway. Most work zones are divided into four areas:

- **Advance warning area**—Where drivers are informed as to what's coming up.

- **Transition area**—Where drivers are redirected to a temporary lane.

- **Activity area**—Where work activity takes place. It includes both a work space where workers, equipment, and material is closed off to traffic, and a traffic space where traffic is routed through the activity area. The activity area may also contain unused buffer spaces to protect both workers and drivers.

- **Termination area**—Where drivers return to their normal lanes.

Where are the regulations?

OSHA rules for work zone safety can be found in §1926.200 to .203—Signs, Signals, and Barricades. Unfortunately, OSHA does not provide much in the way of protecting workers from the hazards of traffic in work zones.

However, while the Department of Transportation (DOT) has the intention of protecting motorists and pedestrians, it also provides some protection for road workers under: 23 CFR 630, Subpart J, Traffic Safety in Highway and Street Work Zones, and 23 CFR 655, Subpart F, Traffic Control Devices on Federal Aid and Other Streets and Highways.

Both OSHA and DOT refer to a national standard for traffic control on all public roads, including work zones. This standard is called the *Manual on Uniform Traffic Control Devices (MUTCD)*.

What are the hazards?

According to the Census of Fatal Occupational Injuries, from 1992 through 1996, 600 highway and street construction workers died. Fifty-five percent of these fatalities were caused by vehicles or equipment. The specific causes of death were:

- Fatalities caused by traffic vehicles totaled 111. Vehicles entering the work space accounted for 104 of these deaths.

- Construction machines or vehicles like dump trucks, rollers, and pavers caused 102 deaths. Of the 102 deaths, 49 involved a backing vehicle.

- Employees operating vehicles or mobile construction equipment accounted for 87 deaths.

Protective measures

While the public traveling through the work zone is important, the focus here is the safety of employees working in the work zone.

Traffic Control Plan

The Traffic Control Plan (TCP) describes the measures used to keep traffic moving safely and efficiently through the work zone. The measures selected depend on the type of roadway, the traffic condition, how long the project will be, location restrictions, and how close the work space is to traffic. A TCP can be very detailed and contain drawings of the particular work zone.

Companies can also create an internal traffic control plan to coordinate the flow of construction vehicles, equipment, and workers operating close to the activity area. When looking at the plan, workers on foot should pay attention to the areas they are not allowed to go into.

Signs

There are three types of traffic control signs:

- **Regulatory signs**—inform roadway users of traffic laws. With some exceptions, these signs are rectangular and black and white. Examples include the STOP, YIELD, DO NOT ENTER, SPEED LIMIT, and ONE WAY signs.

- **Warning signs**—notify drivers of conditions. With some exceptions, these signs are diamond-shaped and orange and black. Examples include the ROAD WORK, DETOUR, ROAD CLOSED, and RIGHT LANE CLOSED signs.

- **Guide signs**—give information to help drivers with, for example, temporary routes, directions, and work being done. These signs are generally orange and black. Examples include the ROAD WORK NEXT # MILES, END ROAD WORK, and DETOUR ARROW signs.

These signs must be visible at all times when work is being done and must be removed or covered when the hazards no longer exist. At night, signs must be retroreflective or illuminated. If signs become worn or damaged, they must be replaced. Generally, signs should be placed on the right-hand side of the roadway.

Other signs found in work zones which do not control traffic include: danger, caution, and exit signs and tags.

Signals

Signals warn of possible or existing hazards. They include:

- Sign paddles or flags held by flaggers.

- Portable changeable message boards.

Other Special Interest Areas

- Flashing arrow displays.

Channelizing devices

Channelizing devices include, but are not limited to: cones, tubular markers, vertical panels, drums, barricades, temporary raised islands, and barriers. These devices protect workers in the work zone, warn and alert drivers to conditions created by roadwork, and guide drivers. Make sure these devices are clean and visible.

Flaggers

When signs, signals, and barricades do not provide enough protection for operations on highways or streets, then flaggers or other traffic controls must be provided. Your company and your flaggers should follow these rules:

- Use red flags (at least 18 inches square) or proper sign paddles when hand signaling in daylight. Most sign paddles have a red STOP sign on one side and an orange SLOW sign on the other. The MUTCD suggests that flags only be used in emergency situations.

- Use red lights when hand signaling at night.

- Use signals that conform to the MUTCD. Here are the signaling methods for sign paddles:

    - **To stop traffic**—Face traffic and hold the STOP sign paddle toward traffic with your arm extended horizontally away from the body. Raise your free arm with your palm toward approaching traffic.

    - **To direct stopped traffic to proceed**—Face traffic and hold the SLOW paddle toward traffic with your arm extended horizontally away from the body. Motion with your free hand for traffic to proceed.

    - **To alert or slow traffic**—Face traffic holding the SLOW paddle toward traffic with your arm extended horizontally away from the body. You may motion up and down with your free hand, palm down, indicating that the vehicle needs to slow down.

- Wear a red or orange vest, shirt, or jacket.

- Wear white pants and a reflectorized vest, shirt, or jacket and a reflectorized hard hat at night.

- Coordinate with other flaggers and communicate by radio if you have no visual contact.

- Know how to combat both heat and cold exposure, dress appropriately, and know where shelter is available.

- Be alert to symptoms associated with carbon monoxide poisoning from vehicular traffic (nausea and headache). If symptoms develop, get to fresh air.

- Use barricades, cones, tubular markers, vertical panels, drums, and barriers to mark areas.

- Be aware of construction equipment around you. In order to know what is approaching from behind, you may need to wear a hard hat mounted mirror, have a buddy "spot" you, or use some kind of motion detector. Equipment operators, too, should know where you are.

Safe work practices

When working near traffic or heavy equipment employees should:

- Wear highly visible clothing and a light-colored hard hat. During the day, wear a vest, shirt, or jacket that is orange, yellow, yellow-green, or a fluorescent version of these colors. At night, the vest, shirt, or jacket must be retroreflective.

- Work where drivers can see them, but as far as possible from traffic. Be aware that drivers may not be able to see employees when the sun is low in the sky or when it is rainy, foggy, or dark.

- Get in and out of traffic spaces and heavy equipment areas quickly and safely.

- Stay alert and don't wear a radio headset.

- Not operate equipment or a vehicle unless they are trained and authorized to operate that equipment. When operating equipment or vehicles employees should:

    - Always wear a seat belt when operating equipment or vehicles.

    - Never move equipment without making visual contact with workers on foot near the equipment.

    - Make sure equipment is inspected daily and that any problems are corrected. Report equipment problems.

    - Use equipment with rollover protective structures.

    - Chock two wheels when leaving equipment.

    - Park where drivers can see them if they must park vehicles near traffic, don't park around blind corners.

Other Work Zone Protective Measures

Other work zone safety precautions and protective measures could include:

- **Temporary barriers**—These devices prevent vehicles from entering areas where hazards, workers, or pedestrians may be.

- **Lower speeds**—If workers are especially vulnerable, work zone engineers should consider lowering the speed of traffic.

- **Shadow vehicle**—If roadwork is mobile, like for pothole patching, a vehicle with proper lights, signs, or a rear impact protector should be used to keep you from being hit.

Other Special Interest Areas

- **Vehicle arresting systems**—This is fencing, cable, or energy absorbing anchors that prevent vehicles from entering activity areas while allowing the vehicle to safely slow down.

- **Rumble strips**—These consist of textured road surfaces that alert drivers to changing conditions.

- **Road closure**—If alternate routes can handle additional traffic, the road may be closed temporarily to give you the greatest protection.

- **Law enforcement**—If you are at high risk, police units may be placed to reduce traffic speeds.

- **Lighting**—To increase visibility at night, the work area and approaches should be well lit. However, floodlights must not create glare for drivers. Low-level truck lights also help operators see workers on foot. Reflective tape or light strips that outline the height and width of construction vehicles and equipment is beneficial.

- **Intrusion warning devices**—These devices may alert you of vehicles that accidentally enter the work space.

Training

Work zone employees must be trained on all aspects of their job, including:

- Their role and location at the site.
- Traffic patterns and heavy equipment operations.
- Recognizing and eliminating or avoiding hazards.
- Understanding flagger signals and safety colors.
- Knowing communication methods and alarms.
- Knowing how to work next to traffic and heavy equipment in a way that minimizes accidents.
- Knowing their escape routes.
- Proper life saving and personal protective equipment.
- Being as visible as possible.
- Knowing how to operate equipment and vehicles and prevent rollovers.

Ultraviolet Radiation

Are your employees at risk?

Did you know that the number of new cases of skin cancer, and the number of deaths caused by the most serious type of skin cancer are rapidly rising in the United States? This is particularly troubling since the numbers for most cancers have been declining. Sunlight is the main source of ultraviolet radiation (UV) known to damage the skin and to cause skin cancer. The amount of UV exposure depends on the strength of the light, the length of exposure, and whether the skin is protected. There are no safe UV rays or safe suntans.

Sun exposure at any age can cause skin cancer. Your skin and eyes are most susceptible to sun damage. You need to be especially careful in the sun if you have:

- Numerous moles, irregular moles, or large moles.
- Freckles or burn before tanning.
- Fair skin, or blond, red, or light brown hair.
- Spend a lot of time outdoors.

Melanoma is the most serious type of skin cancer, and accounts for more than 75 percent of the deaths due to skin cancer. In addition to skin cancer, sun exposure can cause premature aging of the skin, wrinkles, cataracts, and other eye problems.

How do you protect your employees from UV radiation?

There are five important steps your employees can take to protect against UV radiation and skin cancer:

Cover up—Wear clothing to protect as much of your skin as possible. Wear clothing that does not transmit visible light. To determine if the clothing will protect you, try this test: Place your hand between the fabric and a light source. If you can see your hand through the fabric, the garment offers little protection against sun exposure.

Use a sunscreen with an SPF of 15 or higher—Experts recommend products with a Sun Protection Factor (SPF) of at least 15. The number of the SPF represents the level of sunburn protection provided by the sunscreen. An SPF 15 blocks out 93% of the burning UV rays; an SPF 30 blocks out 97% of the burning UV rays. Products labeled "broad spectrum" block both UVB and UVA radiation. Both UVA and UVB contribute to skin cancer.

Apply sunscreen liberally at least 15 minutes before going outside. Reapply every 2 hours or more frequently if you sweat a lot or are swimming.

Warning: Do not depend on sunscreens alone. Combine sunscreen with wide-brimmed hats, UV-protective sunglasses, and tightly woven clothing to increase your protection against UV radiation.

Other Special Interest Areas

Wear a hat—A wide brim hat is ideal because it protects the neck, ears, eyes, forehead, nose, and scalp. A baseball cap provides some protection for the front and top of the head, but not for the back of the neck or the ears where skin cancers commonly develop.

Wear sunglasses that block UV rays—UV-absorbent sunglasses can help protect your eyes from sun damage. Ideal sunglasses do not have to be expensive, but they should block 99 to 100% of UVA and UVB radiation. Check the label to make sure they do. Darker glasses are not necessarily the best. UV protection comes from an invisible chemical applied to the lenses, not from the color or darkness of the lenses.

Limit direct sun exposure—UV rays are most intense when the sun is high in the sky, between 10 AM and 4 PM. If you are unsure about the sun's intensity, take the shadow test: If your shadow is shorter than you, the sun's rays are the strongest. Seek shade whenever possible.

You may also want to check the UV Index for your area. The UV Index usually can be found in the local newspaper or on TV and radio news broadcasts. It gives the expected noon-time UV radiation reaching the earth's surface on a scale of 1 to 10+. It is forecast daily for 58 cities. The higher the number, the greater the exposure to UV radiation. The Index helps determine when to avoid sun exposure and when to take extra protective measures. (See http://www.nws.noaa.gov/om/uvi.htm.)

Should you and your employees get checked?

Yes. Skin cancers detected early can almost always be cured. The most important warning sign for skin cancer is a spot on the skin that is changing in size, shape, or color over a period of 1 month to 1-2 years. The most common skin cancers—basal cell and squamous cell—often take the form of a pale, wax-like, pearly nodule; a red scaly, sharply outlined patch; or a sore that does not heal; whereas melanoma often starts as a small, mole-like growth. So it's important that you examine your body, and see a health care clinician if you find an unusual skin change.

How can you learn more about preventing skin cancer?

There are many websites with good information about preventing, detecting, and treating skin cancer, including the following:

American Cancer Society for melanoma and nonmelanoma skin cancers (scroll menu of common cancers) at http://www.cancer.org, or call (800) ACS-2345.

Centers for Disease Control and Prevention, for various health materials including skin cancer at http://www.cdc.gov/ChooseYourCover, or call (888) 842-6355.

Heat and Cold Stress Equation

Heat stress equation

High temperature + High humidity + Physical work = Heat illness

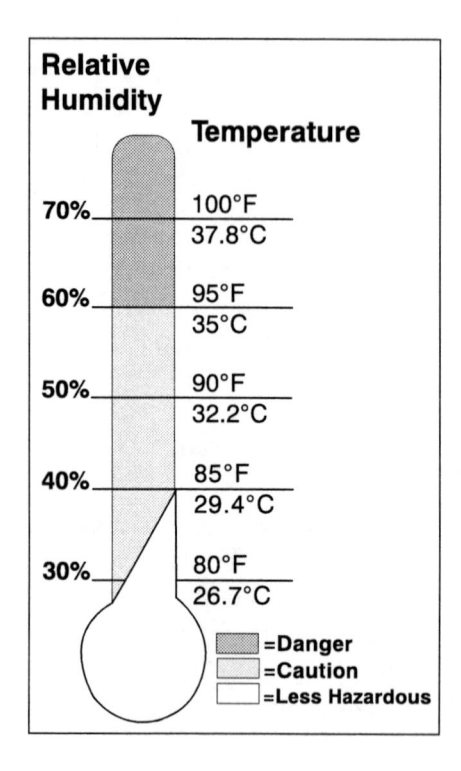

```
Relative
Humidity
              Temperature

70%____        100°F
               37.8°C

60%____        95°F
               35°C

50%____        90°F
               32.2°C

40%____        85°F
               29.4°C

30%____        80°F
               26.7°C

               ▓▓ = Danger
               ▒▒ = Caution
               ☐ = Less Hazardous
```

When the body is unable to cool itself through sweating, serious heat illness may occur. The most severe heat induced illnesses are heat exhaustion and heat stroke. If actions are not taken to treat heat exhaustion, the illness could progress to heat stroke and possible death.

Heat exhaustion

What happens to the body?

- Headaches.
- Dizziness/light headedness.
- Weakness, mood changes (irritable, or confused/can't think straight).
- Feeling sick to your stomach.
- Vomiting/throwing up.

Other Special Interest Areas

- Decreased and dark colored urine.
- Fainting/passing out.
- Pale clammy skin.

What should be done?
- Move your employee to a cool shaded area to rest. Don't leave him alone. If he is dizzy or light headed, lay him on his back and raise his legs about 6-8 inches. If your employee is sick to his stomach lay him on his side.
- Loosen and remove any heavy clothing.
- Have your employee drink some cool water (a small cup every 15 minutes) if he is not feeling sick to his stomach.
- Try to cool your employee by fanning him. Cool the skin with a cool spray mist of water or wet cloth.
- If he does not feel better in a few minutes call for emergency help (ambulance or call 911).
- If heat exhaustion is not treated, the illness may advance to heat stroke.

Heat stroke—A medical emergency

What happens to the body?
- Dry pale skin (no sweating).
- Hot red skin (looks like a sunburn).
- Mood changes (irritable, confused/not making any sense).
- Seizures/fits.
- Collapsed/passed out (will not respond).

What should be done?
- Call for emergency help (ambulance or call 911).
- Move the worker to a cool shaded area. Don't leave your employee alone. Lay him on his back and if he is having seizures/fits remove any objects close to him so he won't strike against them. If your employee is sick to his stomach lay him on his side.
- Remove any heavy and outer clothing.
- Have your employee drink some cool water (a small cup every 15 minutes) if he is alert enough to drink anything and not feeling sick to his stomach.

- Try to cool your employee by fanning him. Cool the skin with a cool spray mist of water, wet cloth, or wet sheet.

- If ice is available, place ice packs under the arm pits and groin area.

How to protect your employees

- Learn the signs and symptoms of heat-induced illnesses and what to do to help your employees.

- Train your employees to recognize and perform first aid measures for heat-induced illnesses.

- Perform your heaviest work in the coolest part of the day.

- Slowly build up heat tolerance and the work activity in your employees (usually takes up to two weeks).

- Use the buddy system (work in pairs).

- Encourage your employees to:

    - Drink plenty of cool water (one small cup every 15-20 minutes).

    - Wear light, loose-fitting breathable clothing. Cotton is a good choice.

    - Take frequent short breaks in cool shaded areas to allow their bodies to cool down.

    - Avoid eating large meals before working in hot environments.

    - Avoid caffeine and alcoholic beverages. Those beverages make the body lose water and increase the risk for heat related illnesses.

Your workers are at increased risk when:

- They take certain medication. You should encourage them to check with their doctor, nurse, or pharmacy and ask if any medicines they are taking affect them when working in hot environments.

- They have had a heat-induced illness in the past.

- They wear personal protective equipment (like respirators or protective suits).

Other Special Interest Areas

Cold stress equation

Low temperature + Wind speed + Wetness = Injuries & illnesses

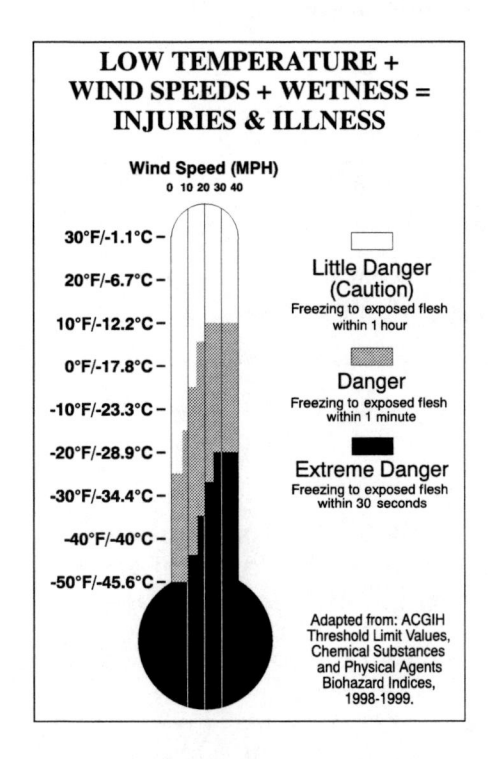

When the body is unable to warm itself, serious cold-related illnesses and injuries may occur, and permanent tissue damage and death may result.

Hypothermia (a medical emergency)

What happens to the body?

- Normal body temperature (98.6°F) drops to or below 95°F.

- Fatigue or drowsiness sets in.

- Uncontrolled shivering.

- Cool bluish skin.

- Slurred speech.

- Clumsy movements.

- Irritable, irrational, or confused behavior.

What should be done (land temperatures)

- **Do not rub the employee's body or place them in a warm water bath. This may stop their heart.**

- Call for emergency help (ambulance or call 911).

- Move the worker to a warm, dry area.

- Don't leave the person alone.

- Remove any wet clothing and replace with warm, dry clothes or wrap the employee in blankets.

- Have the employee drink warm, sweet drinks (sugar water or sports-type drinks) if they are alert. Avoid drinks with caffeine (coffee, tea, or hot chocolate) or alcohol.

- Have the employee move their arms and legs to create muscle heat. If they are unable to do this, place warm bottles or hot packs in the arm pits, groin, neck, and head areas.

What should be done (water temperatures)

- **DO NOT remove any clothing. Button, buckle, zip, and tighten any collars, cuffs, shoes, and hoods because the layer of trapped water closest to the body provides a layer of insulation that slows the loss of heat.**

- Call for emergency help (ambulance or call 911). Body heat is lost up to 25 times faster in water.

- Keep the head out of the water and put on a hat or hood.

- Get out of the water as quickly as possible or climb on anything floating.

- DO NOT attempt to swim unless a floating object or another person can be reached because swimming or other physical activity uses the body's heat and reduces survival time by about 50 percent.

- If getting out of the water is not possible, wait quietly and conserve body heat by folding arms across the chest, keeping thighs together, bending knees, and crossing ankles. If another person is in the water, huddle with chests held closely together.

Frost bite

What happens to the body?

- Freezing in deep layers of skin and tissue.

- Pale, waxy-white skin color.

- Skin becomes hard and numb.

- Usually affects the fingers, hands, toes, feet, ears, and nose.

Other Special Interest Areas

What should be done (land temperatures)

- Move the worker to a warm dry area.

- Don't leave the person alone.

- DO NOT rub the affected area, because rubbing causes damage to the skin and tissue.

- If there is a chance the affected area may get cold again, do not warm the skin. If the skin is warmed and then becomes cold again, it will cause severe tissue damage.

- Remove any wet or tight clothing that may cut off blood flow to the affected area.

- Gently place the affected area in a warm (105°F) water bath and monitor the water temperature to **slowly** warm the tissue. Don't pour warm water directly on the affected area because it will warm the tissue too fast causing tissue damage. Warming takes about 25-40 minutes.

- After the affected area has been warmed, it may become puffy and blister. The affected area may have a burning feeling or numbness.

- When normal feeling, movement, and skin color have returned, dry and wrap the affected area to keep it warm.

- Seek medical attention as soon as possible.

Your employees are at increased risk when they:

- Are wearing inadequate or wet clothing.

- Have predisposing health conditions such as cardiovascular disease, diabetes, and hypertension.

- Are in poor physical condition, have a poor diet, or are older.

- Take certain medication (workers should check with their doctor, nurse, or pharmacy and ask if any medicines they are taking affect them while working in cold environments).

How to protect your employees from cold-related illness and/or injuries

Instruct them to:

- Recognize the environmental and worksite conditions that lead to potential cold-induced illnesses and injuries.

- Learn the signs and symptoms of cold-induced illnesses/injuries and what to do to help a fellow employee.

- Select proper clothing for cold, wet, and windy conditions.

- Layer clothing to adjust to changing environmental temperatures. Wear a hat and gloves, in addition to underwear that will keep water away from the skin (polypropylene).

- Avoid exhaustion or fatigue. Energy is needed to keep muscles warm.

- Use the buddy system (work in pairs).

- Drink warm, sweet beverages (sugar water, sports-type drinks). Avoid drinks with caffeine (coffee, tea, or hot chocolate) or alcohol.

- Eat warm, high-calorie foods like hot pasta dishes.

Allow them to:

- Take frequent short breaks in warm dry shelters to allow the body to warm up.

- Work during the warmest part of the day.

When all precautions fail, and when the body is unable to warm itself, serious cold-related illness and injuries may occur, and permanent tissue damage and death may result. The following information is vital if an employee gets into trouble while working outdoors during cold weather.

Related Regulations for Construction

In addition to OSHA, there are other agencies, such as the Environmental Protection Agency (EPA), that have rules that may be of concern to you. Some of the regulations that could have significance for construction companies are summarized below. Regulatory topics summarized are:

- Asbestos (EPA)
- Lead (EPA)
- Stormwater (EPA)
- Wetlands (EPA)
- Community Right to Know (EPA)
- Hazardous Waste (EPA)
- Americans with Disabilities Act (EEOC)
- Fair Labor Standards Act—Child Labor Provisions (DOL)
- Family and Medical Leave Act (DOL)
- Employment Discrimination in Construction (DOL)
- Wage, Hour and Fringe Benefit Standards for Construction Contracts (DOL)
- Kickbacks in Federally Funded Construction (DOL)

Asbestos (EPA)

EPA's rules in 40 CFR Part 61, Subpart M concerning the application, removal, and disposal of asbestos containing material (ACM), as well as manufacturing, spraying and fabricating of ACM, were issued under the asbestos NESHAP (National Emission Standards for Hazardous Air Pollutants). The asbestos NESHAP regulation governs asbestos demolition and renovation projects in all facilities. The NESHAP rule usually requires owners or operators to have all friable ACM removed before a building is demolished, and may require its removal before a renovation.

For renovation projects where friable ACM will be disturbed, the NESHAP rule may require appropriate work practices or procedures for the control of emissions.

- EPA or the state (if the state has been delegated authority under NESHAP) must be notified before a building containing ACM is demolished or renovated. The notification requirements do not apply if a building owner plans renovation projects which will disturb less than the NESHAP limits of 160 square feet of friable ACM on facility components or 260 linear feet of friable ACM on pipes (quantities involved over a one-year period). For renovation operations in which the amount of ACM equals or exceeds the NESHAP limits, notification is required as soon as possible.

- The NESHAP asbestos rule prohibits visible emissions to the outside air by requiring emission control procedures and appropriate work practices during collection, packaging, transportation or disposal of friable ACM waste. All ACM must be kept wet until sealed in a leak-tight container that includes the appropriate label.

- Under expanded authority of RCRA, a few states have classified asbestos-containing waste as a hazardous waste, and require stringent handling, manifesting, and disposal procedures. In those cases, the state hazardous waste agency should be contacted before disposing of asbestos for approved disposal methods and recordkeeping requirements, and for a list of approved disposal sites.

  Friable asbestos is also included as a hazardous substance under EPA's CERCLA regulations. The owner or manager of a facility (e.g., building, installation, vessel, landfill) may have some reporting requirements.

Lead (EPA)

In an effort to protect families from exposure to the hazards of lead-based paint, Congress amended the Toxic Substances Control Act (TSCA) in 1992 to add Title IV, entitled Lead Exposure Reduction. Title IV of TSCA directs EPA to address the general public's risk of exposure to lead-based paint hazards through regulations, education, and other activities.

Distribution of lead hazard pamphlet

One particular concern of Congress and EPA is the potential lead exposure risks that can occur during renovations of housing containing lead-based paint unless certain safety measures are taken. When lead-based paint is disturbed during renovation, it may contaminate dust and soil, posing hazards, especially to young children.

Recognizing that many families might be unaware that their homes might contain lead-based paint, EPA developed a lead hazard information pamphlet entitled *Protect Your Family From Lead In Your Home*. This pamphlet provides families with prevention tips on reducing exposure to lead hazards from various sources.

As of June 1, 1999, EPA's final rule (40 CFR 745 Subpart E) requires renovators to give homeowners and tenants the pamphlet before beginning renovation activities in pre-1978 housing. It is estimated that 80 percent of all residential dwellings built before 1978 contain some lead-based paint.

Related Regulations for Construction

The regulation does not apply to renovation activities that are limited to the following:

- Minor repair and maintenance activities (including minor electrical work and plumbing) that disrupt 2 square feet or less of painted surface per component.
- Emergency renovation operations.
- Renovation activities that take place in housing that has already been determined by a certified inspector to be lead free.

Information distribution requirements

No more than 60 days before beginning renovation activities in any residential dwelling unit of target housing, the renovator must provide the owner of the unit with the pamphlet, and comply with one of the following:

- Obtain, from the owner, a written acknowledgment that the owner has received the pamphlet.
- Obtain a certificate of mailing at least 7 days prior to the renovation.

In addition, if the owner does not occupy the dwelling unit, the renovator must provide an adult occupant of the unit with the pamphlet, and comply with one of the following:

- Obtain, from the adult occupant, a written acknowledgment that the occupant has received the pamphlet; or certify in writing that a pamphlet has been delivered to the dwelling and that the renovator has been unsuccessful in obtaining a written acknowledgment from an adult occupant.
- Obtain a certificate of mailing at least 7 days prior to the renovation.

When renovating common areas of multi-family housing, the renovator must notify in writing, or ensure written notification of, each unit of the multi-family housing and make the pamphlet available upon request prior to the start of renovation.

Recordkeeping requirements

Renovators must retain and, if requested, make available to EPA all records necessary to demonstrate compliance for a period of 3 years following completion of the renovation activities including:

- Reports certifying that a determination had been made by an inspector that lead-based paint is not present in the area affected by the renovation.
- Signed and dated acknowledgments of receipt of the pamphlet.
- Certifications of attempted delivery of the pamphlet.
- Certificates of mailing the pamphlet.
- Records of notification activities performed regarding common area renovations.

Enforcement and inspections

Failure or refusal to comply with any provision of this regulation is a violation of TSCA, and violators may be subject to civil and criminal sanctions for each violation. EPA may conduct inspections and issue subpoenas to ensure compliance with this subpart.

Accreditation and certification (target housing and child-occupied facilities)

EPA's regulations in 40 CFR 745 Subpart L ensure that contractors claiming to know how to inspect, assess, or remove lead-based paint, dust or soil are well qualified, trained and certified to conduct these activities.

Subpart L contains:

- Procedures and requirements for the accreditation of lead-based paint activities training programs.

- Procedures and requirements for the certification of individuals and firms engaged in lead-based paint activities.

- Work practice standards for performing such activities.

This subpart also requires that all lead-based paint activities (with a few exceptions) be performed by certified individuals and firms.

Accreditation of training programs

A training program may seek accreditation to offer lead-based paint activities courses (and refresher courses) in any of the following disciplines: inspector, risk assessor, supervisor, project designer, and abatement worker.

A training program must not provide, offer, or claim to provide EPA-accredited lead-based paint activities courses without applying for and receiving accreditation. Accredited training programs shall maintain and make available to EPA, upon request, specific records. Unless re-accredited, a training program's accreditation shall expire 4 years after the date of issuance.

Certification of individuals

Individuals seeking certification by EPA to engage in lead-based paint activities as an inspector, risk assessor, supervisor, project designer, or abatement worker must meet requirements found in §745.226(b) and (c).

Any individual who received training in a lead-based paint activity between October 1, 1990, and March 1, 1999, will be eligible for certification by EPA under alternative procedures found in §745.226(d).

Related Regulations for Construction

To maintain certification in a particular discipline, a certified individual must apply to and be recertified by EPA in that discipline either:

- Every 3 years if the individual completed a training course with a course test and hands-on assessment; or
- Every 5 years if the individual completed a training course with a proficiency test.

Certification of firms

A firm seeking certification shall submit to EPA a letter attesting that the firm shall only employ appropriately certified employees, and that the firm and its employees shall follow the work practice standards in §745.227.

From the date of receiving the firm's letter requesting certification, EPA shall have 90 days to approve or disapprove the firm's request for certification. Within that time, EPA shall respond with either a certificate of approval or a letter describing the reasons for a disapproval.

Fees

As specified in TSCA, training programs, individuals and firms must submit the appropriate fees in accordance with §745.238 when applying for and renewing accreditation or certification. No fee shall be imposed on any training program operated by a State, federally recognized Indian Tribe, local government, or nonprofit organization.

Work practice standards for conducting lead-based paint activities

Section 745.227 requires that only EPA-certified individuals and firms conduct the following lead-based paint activities according to established work practices:

Inspection

- Selecting areas to be tested for the presence of lead-based paint.
- Sampling paint.
- Writing an inspection report.

Lead-hazard screen

- Collecting background information.
- Conducting a visual inspection.
- Testing paint for the presence of lead.
- Collecting and analyzing dust samples.
- Sampling paint.
- Preparing a lead hazard screen report.

Risk assessment

- Conducting a visual inspection.
- Collecting background information.
- Testing paint for the presence of lead.
- Collecting and analyzing dust and soil samples.
- Preparing a risk assessment report.

Abatement

- Ensuring presence of a certified supervisor.
- Notifying EPA of the commencement of abatement activities.
- Developing a written occupant protection plan.
- Restricting certain work practices such as open-flame burning and machine sanding.
- Removing or covering lead-contaminated soil.
- Performing post-abatement clearance procedures.
- Preparing an abatement report and maintaining records.

Violations

As of March 1, 2000, it is a violation of TSCA for individuals and firms **NOT** certified by EPA to conduct the lead-based paint activities described in §745.227. EPA may, after notice and opportunity for hearing, suspend, revoke, or modify the certification of a training program, an individual or a firm if specific provisions of the regulation are violated.

Stormwater (EPA)

In an effort to address some of the problems associated with diffuse or nonpoint pollution sources, Congress passed the Water Quality Act of 1987. The Act required the EPA to establish regulations (40 CFR Part 122) setting forth phased National Pollutant Discharge Elimination System (NPDES) stormwater permit requirements. The stormwater program consists of two phases.

Phase I requires permits for:

- Stormwater discharges associated with industrial activity (including construction activities such as clearing, grading, and excavations, EXCEPT operations that result in the

Related Regulations for Construction

disturbance of less than five acres of total land area which are not part of a larger common plan of development or sale).

- Discharges from large municipal separate storm sewer systems (those serving a population of 250,000 or more).

- Discharges from medium municipal separate storm sewer systems (those serving populations of between 100,000 and 250,000).

Phase II requires permits for:

- Discharges from regulated small municipal separate stormwater systems (*regulated* means located in urbanized areas as defined by the Bureau of Census and *small* means any not already covered by Phase I).

- Stormwater discharges associated with construction activities that disturb equal to or greater than 1 and less than 5 acres of land.

Waivers from coverage are available. Additional small municipal systems (outside urbanized areas) and construction sites (disturbing less than 1 acre of land) may be brought into the NPDES Stormwater Program by the NPDES permitting authority case-by-case. Phase II became final November 1999 and it supercedes the interim Phase II Direct Final Rule published in 1995.

Permit application

Facilities engaging in construction activities may either apply for an individual stormwater permit or for a general stormwater permit.

- **Individual permits** are for facilities that choose to file individually or have been disqualified from a group permit.

- **General permits** will be the most common permit option and will apply to a particular class of dischargers.

EPA has set forth distinct individual permit application requirements for construction activities at §122.26(c)(1), to be used where general permits are inapplicable. Facilities applying for an individual permit are required to provide a map indicating the site's location, the name of the receiving water and a narrative description of:

- The nature of the construction activity.

- The total area of the site and the area of the site expected to undergo excavation during the life of the permit.

- Proposed measures, including best management practices, to control pollutants in stormwater discharges during construction, including a description of applicable federal requirements and state or local erosion and sediment control requirements.

- Proposed measures to control pollutants in stormwater discharges that will occur after construction operations have been completed, including a description of applicable state and local erosion and sediment control requirements.

- An estimate of the runoff coefficient (fraction of total rainfall that will appear as runoff) of the site and the increase in impervious area after the construction addressed in the permit application is completed.

- A description of the nature of fill material, and existing data describing the soil or the quality of the discharge.

Individual permit application requirements for construction activities do not include the submission of quantitative data.

The application deadline for stormwater discharge permits for construction activities is at least 90 days prior to the date the construction is to commence.

Notice of intent

Regulations for general permits require industrial dischargers eligible for a general permit to submit a Notice of Intent (NOI) with the regional EPA administrator or, if the state has a state NPDES program, the state director.

The regulations require the contents of the NOI to be specified in the general permit and to include, at a minimum, the following information:

- The legal name and address of the owner or operator.
- The facility name and address.
- The type of facility or discharge.
- The name of the receiving water or waters.

The general permit will specify when a discharger is authorized to discharge, either upon filing the NOI, after a specified waiting period, on a specified date, or upon receipt of notification of inclusion by the Director.

Monitoring

The regulation provides for monitoring reports for stormwater discharges to be required on a case-by-case basis with frequency dependent upon the nature and effect of the discharge. At a minimum, a permit for stormwater discharges associated with industrial activity must require:

- The discharger to conduct an annual inspection of the facility site to identify areas contributing to a stormwater discharge and to evaluate whether measures to reduce pollutant loadings are adequate and properly implemented or whether additional control measures are needed.

Related Regulations for Construction

- The discharger to maintain records, for a period of three years, summarizing the inspection results, certifying the facility is in compliance with the permit and the stormwater pollution prevention plan, and identifying any incidents of noncompliance.

Best management practices

In addition to applying for permits, covered operators must also implement stormwater discharge management controls (often referred to as best management practices or BMPs), as applicable, that effectively reduce or prevent the discharge of pollutants into receiving waters.

For more information

For more detailed information on the Phase I and Phase II stormwater permitting process, go to EPA's Office of Wastewater Management website at http://www.epa.gov/owm/sw.

Wetlands (EPA)

Section 404 of the Clean Water Act establishes a program which requires a Federal permit to discharge dredged or fill materials into waters of the United States, including wetlands.

Wetlands are areas that are inundated or saturated by surface or groundwater at a frequency or duration sufficient to support, and that under normal circumstances do support, a prevalence of vegetation typically adapted for life in saturated soil conditions. Wetlands generally include swamps, marshes, bogs, estuaries, and other inland and coastal areas. Fill material is any material which changes the bottom elevation of a water body for any purpose.

Activities regulated under the Section 404 program include:

- Placement of fill that is necessary for the construction of any structure in a water of the United States.

- The building of any structure or impoundment requiring rock, sand, dirt or other material for its construction.

- Site-development fills for recreational, industrial, commercial, residential, and other uses.

The Army Corps of Engineers (Corps) and EPA, who jointly administer the program, issue permits for these activities after evaluating the application for a variety of criteria including the impacts on fish and wildlife, the duration and extent of the proposed action, the effect on water quality and the availability of alternative measures.

Permits

Regulated activities are controlled by a permit review process. The basic premise of the program is that no discharge of dredged or fill material can be permitted if a practicable alternative exists that is less damaging to the aquatic environment or if the nation's waters would be significantly degraded. In other words, when you apply for a permit, you must show that you have:

- Taken steps to avoid wetland impacts where practicable.

- Minimized potential impacts to wetlands.

- Provided compensation for any remaining, unavoidable impacts through activities to restore or create wetlands.

General permits—For most discharges that will have only minimal adverse effects, the Corps often grants up-front general permits. These may be issued on a nationwide, regional, or state basis for particular categories of activities (for example, minor road crossings, utility line backfill, and bedding) as a means to expedite the permitting process. A general permit can be granted if:

- The activities in such category are similar in nature and similar in their impact upon water quality and aquatic environment.

- The activities in such category will have only minimal adverse effects when performed separately.

- The activities in such category will have only minimal cumulative adverse effects on water quality and the aquatic environment.

Individual permits—An individual permit is usually required for potentially significant impacts. The 404 individual permit process includes the following steps: (1) public notice (describing the proposed activity, its location, and potential environmental impacts) is issued by the Corps, (2) a 15-30 day comment period is held, (3) citizens may request a public hearing, (4) the Corps conducts a permit evaluation, and (5) an Environmental Assessment and Statement of Finding, which explains how the permit decision was made, is made available to the public.

Denying a disposal site

EPA is authorized to prohibit or otherwise restrict a site whenever they determine that the discharge of dredged or fill material is having or will have an "unacceptable adverse effect" on municipal water supplies, shellfish beds and fishery areas (including spawning and breeding areas), wildlife, or recreational areas. In making this determination, EPA will take into account all information available and will consult with the Corps or with the state.

Regulations establishing procedures to be followed by the EPA in denying or restricting a disposal site appear at 40 CFR Part 231. The process includes the administrator's proposed determination, public notice of the proposed determination, 30-60 day comment period, a

Related Regulations for Construction

possible public hearing, new recommended determination (with possible corrective actions) or withdrawal of proposed determination, and final determination.

Agency responsibilities

The Army Corps of Engineers:

- Administers the day-to-day program, including individual permit decisions and jurisdictional determinations.

- Develops policy and guidance.

- Enforces Section 404 provisions.

The Environmental Protection Agency:

- Develops and interprets environmental criteria used in evaluating permit applications (40 CFR Part 230).

- Determines scope of geographic jurisdiction.

- Approves and oversees State assumption.

- Identifies activities that are exempt.

- Reviews/comments on individual permit applications.

- Has authority to veto the Corps' permit decisions (Section 404(c)).

- Can elevate specific cases (Section 404(q)).

- Enforces Section 404 provisions.

Note: For more in depth information on wetlands and a new proposed rule affecting the definition of "discharge of dredged material," see EPA's website at www.epa.gov/owow/wetlands.

Community Right To Know (EPA)

The Superfund Amendments and Reauthorization Act (SARA), Title III, was developed in 1987 by EPA to address concerns that communities have over the possibilities of emergencies due to the in-plant storage and/or release of hazardous chemicals.

SARA, also known as Community Right To Know (40 CFR Parts 355, 370, and 372), is a complicated collection of regulations that establishes new authorities for emergency planning and preparedness, emergency release notification, community right to know reporting, and toxic chemical release reporting.

SARA requires companies to report what hazardous substances they have in-plant or on-site and to provide safety and health information related to these substances. The data is intended to help communities focus on the substances and facilities of the most immediate concern for emergency planning and response.

Right to know reporting

Any facility which must prepare or have available materials safety data sheets (MSDSs) under OSHA's Hazard Communication Standard must comply with the following requirements.

- A Tier I form must be filed listing all hazardous chemicals that you have 10,000 pounds or more of, now or at any time during the preceding year; and any of the Extremely Hazardous Substances listed in Part 355 of the regulation in amounts over 500 pounds (or 55 gallons) or the threshold planning quantity, whichever is less.

  For most companies, this information was first submitted on March 1, 1988, and then annually, thereafter. The Tier I or Tier II submission deadline is March 1 annually.

- MSDSs for all hazardous chemicals must be submitted to local emergency planning committees, state commissions, and local fire departments. Updates must be submitted to these agencies within three months after a new MSDS or a significant change is added.

  As an alternative to submitting MSDSs, a list of regulated chemicals can be developed and submitted.

- A Tier II form, which requires specific information on each hazardous chemical at the facility or site, a description of its storage, and the exact location of the hazardous chemical, must be submitted only upon request from the local emergency planning committee, state commissions, and/or local fire departments. Tier II forms must be submitted within 30 days of the receipt of such request.

  Some states require automatic filing of Tier II forms. Check with your state agency for details.

Emergency planning and release notification

Any facility which has any one of EPA's designated Extremely Hazardous Substances or a CERCLA hazardous substance present in a regulated amount must comply with the requirements of this section.

EPA's List of Extremely Hazardous Substances and Their Threshold Planning Quantities is found in 40 CFR Part 355, Appendix A and Appendix B. The CERCLA List of Hazardous Substances and Reportable Quantities is found in Section 302.4.

- Your state emergency response commission must be notified that your facility is subject to the requirements of this section.

Related Regulations for Construction

- If you start using, producing, or storing an extremely hazardous substance and have never provided notification under this section, you must report within 60 days that your facility is now subject to these requirements.

- A facility emergency coordinator must be designated for all regulated companies. The owner/operator of each company must appoint a coordinator who will cooperate with local committees. Local emergency response committees should be notified as to who the coordinator is.

- Local committees must be informed of any changes occurring at your facility which may be relevant to emergency planning. Any request by the local committees for information necessary for the development of the local emergency plan should be promptly complied with.

- Companies must provide emergency notification whenever there is a release of a Reportable Quantity of any Extremely Hazardous Substance or CERCLA hazardous substance. "Release" is defined as any spilling, leaking, pumping, pouring, emptying, discharging, or disposing into the environment. This includes the abandonment or discarding of barrels or other closed receptacles. Any release which results in exposure to persons solely within the boundaries of your facility does not require notification under this regulation.

Immediate notification must be made to: 1) the community emergency coordinator of the local committee, and 2) the state commission for any area which may be affected by the release. This notification should be oral (via telephone, radio, or in person).

Hazardous Waste (EPA)

In 1976, Congress passed the Resource Conservation and Recovery Act (RCRA) which directed EPA to develop and implement a program to protect human health and the environment from improper hazardous waste management. The program is designed to control the management of hazardous waste from its generation to its ultimate disposal—from "cradle to grave."

What Is hazardous waste?

There are two ways for a waste to be considered hazardous:

- It can be specifically listed as hazardous in one of four lists found in the RCRA regulations (40 CFR Part 261).

- It can possess one of the four characteristics of hazardous waste—ignitable, corrosive, reactive or toxic.

There is also a separate category of hazardous waste considered to be "acutely hazardous." These are wastes that are so dangerous in small amounts that they are regulated the same way as large amounts of other hazardous wastes.

If your business doesn't produce waste that meets the criteria listed above, you do not need to be concerned with EPA's hazardous waste regulations (40 CFR Parts 260-268). However, if your business does produce hazardous waste, you must determine which generator classification you fall under and comply with the appropriate regulations.

Generator categories

EPA defines three categories of hazardous waste generators based upon the quantity of hazardous waste they generate per month. They are:

- Conditionally exempt small quantity generators (CESQGs), which generate less than 220 lbs (100 kg) per month.

- Small quantity generators (SQGs), which generate between 220 lbs (100 kg) and 2,200 (1,000 kg) per month.

- Large quantity generators (LQGs), which generate more than 2,200 lbs (1,000 kg) per month.

To determine which category your business is in, measure wastes that are:

- Accumulated on the property for any period of time before disposal or recycling. (Dry cleaners, for example, must count any residue removed from machines, as well as spent cartridge filters.)

- Packaged and transported away from your business.

- Placed directly in a regulated treatment or disposal unit at your place of business.

- Generated as still bottoms or sludges and removed from product storage tanks.

DO NOT measure wastes that:

- Are specifically exempted from counting. Examples include lead-acid batteries that will be reclaimed, scrap metal that will be recycled, used oil managed under the used oil provisions of 40 CFR 279, and universal wastes (e.g., batteries, pesticides, lamps and thermostats) managed under 40 CFR 273.

- Might be left in the bottom of containers that have been thoroughly emptied through conventional means such as pouring or pumping.

- Are left as residue in the bottom of tanks storing products, if the residue is not removed from the product tank.

- Are reclaimed continuously on site without storing prior to reclamation, such as dry cleaning solvents.

Related Regulations for Construction

- Are managed in an elementary neutralization unit, a totally enclosed treatment unit, or a wastewater treatment unit, without being stored first.

- Are discharged directly to publicly owned treatment works (POTWs) without being stored or accumulated first. This discharge to a POTW must comply with the Clean Water Act. POTWs are public utilities, usually owned by the city, county, or state, that treat industrial and domestic sewage for disposal.

- Have already been counted once during the calendar month, and are treated on site or reclaimed in some manner, and used again.

- Are regulated under the universal waste rule or have other special requirements. The federal regulations contain special, limited requirements for managing certain commonly generated wastes. These wastes can be managed following the less burdensome requirements instead of the usual hazardous waste requirements. [Used oil—40 CFR Part 279; Lead-acid batteries that are reclaimed—40 CFR Part 266, Subpart G; Scrap metal that is recycled—40 CFR 261.6 (a)(3); Universal wastes (e.g., certain batteries, recalled and collected pesticides, mercury-containing thermostats and lamps)—40 CFR Part 273]

Once you have determined which category of generator your business is, you will need to comply with the hazardous waste rules specific to that category regarding:

- EPA identification numbers
- Manifests
- Packaging
- Labeling
- Marking
- Placarding
- Accumulation time
- Recordkeeping and reporting

Americans with Disabilities Act (EEOC)

The Americans with Disabilities Act (ADA), 29 CFR Part 1630 and 28 CFR Part 36, was signed into law on July 26, 1990. Title I of the ADA is enforced by the Equal Employment Opportunity Commission (EEOC). It is a federal anti-discrimination statute designed to make both public and private entities accessible to the 43 million disabled Americans across the country. The statute prohibits discrimination against disabled Americans based upon their disability and places the burden for reasonably accommodating their special needs on employers, retail establishments, service entities, and others. The ultimate goal of the law is to allow Americans with disabilities to lead productive lives by providing, in general, minor accommodations to accomplish this goal.

The Act itself is divided into five sections or titles. Each title addresses a different aspect of discrimination against the disabled. Title I addresses discrimination in employment. Title II prohibits state and local governments from discriminating in their employment policies and in the administration and delivery of their services or programs. Discrimination in places of public accommodation is banned in Title III, requiring buildings, services, and communications within buildings and facilities to be accessible to the disabled. Title IV deals with the accessibility issues relative to telecommunication services. Title V covers miscellaneous issues. Titles I and III are of the most interest to businesses and employers, because these sections have the greatest impact on day-to-day operations.

The following points briefly summarize the provisions of Titles I and III.

Title I

- No employer, employment agency, labor organization, or joint labor-management committee shall discriminate against a qualified individual with a disability because of the disability of such individual in regard to job application procedures, the hiring, advancement, or discharge of employees, employee compensation, job training, and other terms, conditions, and privileges of employment.

- It is unlawful for employers to limit, segregate, or classify a job applicant or employee in a way that adversely affects the opportunities or status of such applicant or employee because of the disability of such applicant or employee.

- Employees with disabilities are to be accorded equal access to whatever health insurance coverage the employer provides to an employee.

- Employers are prohibited from participating in a contractual or other arrangement or relationship that has the effect of subjecting an employer's qualified applicant employee with a disability to the discrimination prohibited by this title. (Such relationship includes a relationship with an employment or referral agency, labor union, an organization providing fringe benefits to an employee of the covered entity, or an organization providing training and apprenticeship programs.)

- Policies and practices that screen out or tend to screen out an individual with a disability or a class of individuals with disabilities are unlawful unless they are job-related and consistent with business necessity.

- All employers with 15 or more employees need to comply with the Act.

Title III

- Places of public accommodation must make reasonable modifications to their policies, practices, and procedures to allow access to the disabled. Places of public accommoda-

Related Regulations for Construction

tion include over five million private establishments, such as restaurants, hotels, theaters, convention centers, retail stores, shopping centers, dry cleaners, laundromats, pharmacies, doctors' offices, hospitals, museums, libraries, parks, zoos, amusement parks, private schools, day care centers, health spas, and bowling alleys.

- Structural and architectural barriers in existing facilities of public accommodation must be removed when it is readily achievable to do so. Readily achievable means "easily accomplishable and able to be carried out without much difficulty or expense." What is readily achievable will be determined on a case-by-case basis in light of the resources available.

- All newly constructed places of public accommodation and commercial facilities (nonresidential facilities, including office buildings, factories, and warehouses, whose operations affect commerce) must be accessible to individuals with disabilities to the extent that it is not structurally impracticable.

- New construction and alterations must be accessible in compliance with the ADA Accessibility Guidelines. The Guidelines contain general design ("technical") standards for building and site elements, such as parking, accessible routes, ramps, stairs, elevators, doors, entrances, drinking fountains, bathrooms, controls and operating mechanisms, storage areas, alarms, signage, telephones, fixed seating and tables, assembly areas, automated teller machines, and dressing rooms. They also have specific technical standards for restaurants, medical care facilities, mercantile facilities, libraries, and transient lodging (such as hotels and shelters).

The Guidelines also contain "scoping" requirements for various elements (i.e., it specifies how many, and under what circumstances, accessibility features must be incorporated).

Fair Labor Standards Act—Child Labor Provisions (DOL)

The Fair Labor Standards Act child labor provisions (29 CFR 570-580) are designed to protect minors by restricting the types of jobs and the number of hours they may work. This Act is administered by the Department of Labor's Employment Standards Administration, Wage and Hour Division.

Prohibited jobs

Seventeen hazardous non-farm jobs, as determined by the Secretary of Labor, are out of bounds for teens below the age of 18. Generally, they may not work at jobs that involve:

- Manufacturing or storing explosives.

- Driving a motor vehicle and being an outside helper on a motor vehicle.

- Coal mining.
- Logging and sawmilling.
- Power-driven wood-working machines.*
- Exposure to radioactive substances and to ionizing radiations.
- Power-driven hoisting equipment.
- Power-driven metal-forming, punching, and shearing machines.*
- Mining, other than coal mining.
- Meat packing or processing (including power-driven meat slicing machines).
- Power-driven bakery machines.
- Power-driven paper-products machines.*
- Manufacturing brick, tile, and related products.
- Power-driven circular saws, band saws, and guillotine shears.*
- Wrecking, demolition, and ship-breaking operations.
- Roofing operations.*
- Excavation operations.*

* Limited exemptions are provided for apprentices and student-learners under specified standards.

Hour limitations

- Youths 18 or older may perform any job, whether hazardous or not, for unlimited hours, in accordance with minimum wage and overtime requirements.
- Youths age 16 and 17 may perform any non-hazardous job, for unlimited hours.
- Youths age 14 and 15 may work outside school hours in various nonmanufacturing, non-mining, nonhazardous jobs up to:
    - 3 hours on a school day.
    - 18 hours in a school week.
    - 8 hours on a non-school day.
    - 40 hours in a non-school week.
- Work must be performed between the hours of 7 a.m. and 7 p.m. (extended to 9 p.m. from June 1 through Labor Day).

Related Regulations for Construction

- Youths enrolled in an approved Work Experience and Career Exploration Program may work up to 23 hours in a school week and 3 hours on a school day (including during school hours).

Requirements

Department of Labor regulations require employers to keep records of their employees under age 19 including their date of birth, starting and quitting times, daily and weekly hours worked, and their occupation. Employers may protect themselves from unintentional violation of the child labor provisions by keeping on file an employment or age certificate for each youth employed to show that the youth is the minimum age for the job. It is a violation of the Act to fire, or in any other manner discriminate against, an employee for filing a complaint or for participating in a legal proceeding under the Act.

Penalties

Employers are subject to a civil money penalty of up to $10,000 for each employee employed in violation of the child labor provisions. When a penalty is assessed, employers have the right, within 15 days of receipt, to file an exception to the determination that will be referred to an administrative law judge for a hearing. Either party may appeal the judge's decision to the Secretary of Labor. If an exception is not filed in a timely manner, the penalty becomes final.

An employer who is convicted of a second offense is subject to a fine of not more than $10,000, imprisonment for up to six months, or both. The Secretary of Labor may also bring suit to obtain injunctions to restrain persons from violating the Act.

Family and Medical Leave Act (DOL)

The Family and Medical Act (FMLA), 29 CFR 825, allows employees to balance their work and family life by taking reasonable unpaid leave for certain family and medical reasons. The Act is administered and enforced by the Department of Labor's Employment Standards Administration, Wage and Hour Division.

Employer coverage

FMLA applies to all:

- Private sector employers who employ 50 or more employees for at least 20 workweeks in the current or preceding calendar year.

- Public agencies, including state, local and federal employers, and local education agencies.

Employee eligibility

To be eligible for FMLA leave, an employee must work for a covered employer and:

- Have worked for that employer for at least 12 months.
- Have worked at least 1,250 hours during the 12 months prior to the start of the FMLA leave.
- Work at a location where at least 50 employees are employed at the location or within 75 miles of the location.

Leave entitlement

A covered employer must grant an eligible employee up to a total of 12 workweeks of unpaid leave in a 12 month period for one or more of the following reasons:

- For the birth of a child, and to care for the newborn child.
- For the placement with the employee of a child for adoption or foster care, and to care for the newly placed child.
- To care for an immediate family member (spouse, child, or parent—but not a parent-in-law) with a serious health condition.
- When the employee is unable to work because of a serious health condition.

Maintenance of health benefits

- A covered employer is required to maintain group health insurance for an employee on leave on the same terms as if the employee continued to work.
- An employer's obligation to maintain health benefits stops when an employee informs the employer of an intent not to return to work or if the employee fails to return to work when the FMLA leave entitlement is exhausted.
- The employer's obligation also stops if the employee's premium payment is more than 30 days late and the employer has given the employee written notice 15 days in advance that coverage will cease if payment is not received.
- In some circumstances, the employer may recover its share of the insurance premiums for an employee who fails to return to work.

Other provisions

- Taking intermittent leave for the birth and care, placement for adoption, or foster care of a child is subject to approval by the employer. Except for leave relating to the pregnancy which would be leave for a serious health condition.

Related Regulations for Construction

- When leave is foreseeable, an employee must provide the employer with at least 30 days notice. If the leave is not foreseeable, then notice must be given as soon as practicable.

- An employer may require medical certification from a health care provider to verify a serious health condition. The employer may also require periodic reports of the employee's status and intent to return to work, as well as "fitness-for-duty" certification upon return to work.

- At the conclusion of the leave, an employee is entitled to return to the same position or a position with equivalent pay, benefits, and working conditions.

Penalties

Employers are required to post a notice for employees that outlines the basic provisions of FMLA and are subject to a civil money penalty for willfully failing to post such notice. Employers are prohibited from discriminating against or interfering with employees who take FMLA leave.

Employees or any person may file complaints with the Employment Standards Administration, U.S. Department of Labor (usually through the nearest office of the Wage and Hour Division). The Secretary may file suit to ensure compliance and recover damages if a complaint cannot be resolved administratively. Employees also have private rights of action without involvement of the Department to correct violations and recover damages through the courts.

Employment Discrimination in Construction (DOL)

Executive Order 11246 and its implementing regulations (41 CFR 60, Parts 1,3,4,20-50), which are administered and enforced by the Department of Labor's Employment Standards Administration, Office of Federal Contract Compliance Programs (OFCCP), protects all on-site construction employees of covered contractors from employment discrimination.

Who is covered

The Executive Order covers employers with federal contracts or subcontracts and federally assisted construction contracts in excess of $10,000. The following types of contracts are exempt from the Executive Order:

- Transactions of $10,000 and under.

- Contracts for work that is performed outside the United States by employees who were not recruited in the U.S.

- Contracts exempt for national interest or security reasons.

Specific exceptions may apply to the following:

- Contracts with certain educational institutions (e.g. religiously oriented church colleges).
- Contracts for work on or near Indian reservations.

Basic provisions/requirements

- The Executive Order prohibits covered employers from discriminating against employees or job applicants because of race, color, religion, sex or national origin and requires them to take affirmative action to ensure equal employment opportunity for these protected groups.

- Covered contractors must strive to meet geographic goals established by the OFCCP for the employment of women and minorities in all crafts and trades in the area.

- Race, color, religion, sex and national origin distinctions may not be made in recruitment or advertising efforts, employment opportunities, wages, hours, job classifications, seniority, retirement ages or job fringe benefits such as employer contributions to company pension or insurance plans.

- Construction contractors must fully document their affirmative action efforts, and shall implement affirmative action steps that are at least as extensive as those listed in 41 CFR 60 Part 4.3.

- Exclusionary policies may not differ between the sexes. For example, an employer cannot deny a job to a woman because she has young children unless the same policy applies to men.

- Lack of appropriate physical facilities may not be a reason for refusing to hire men or women, unless the employer can prove undue hardship such as excessive expense in providing reasonable accommodations. Employers also may not depend on State "protective" laws to deny employment to a qualified female applicant.

- Covered employers are required to comply with the Pregnancy Discrimination Act of 1978. They must provide equal fringe benefits and make equal contributions for such benefits for men and women.

- Sexual harassment is a violation of the nondiscrimination provisions of the Executive Order.

- Employers are required to take all necessary actions to ensure that no one attempts to intimidate or discriminate against an individual for filing a complaint or participating in a proceeding under the Executive Order.

Related Regulations for Construction

Penalties

OFCCP investigates for violations of the Executive Order either through compliance reviews or in response to complaints. If a violation is found after an investigation, the Federal contractor is asked to enter into conciliation negotiations. If conciliation efforts fail, OFCCP initiates an administrative enforcement proceeding by issuing an administrative complaint to the contractor.

The contractor has 20 days to request a review by an administrative law judge, who hears the case and makes a determination. The contractor may appeal this judge's decision to the Administrative Review Board of the Department of Labor and, if dissatisfied with its decision, to the Federal courts.

Violations may result in withholding of proposed contracts, canceling, suspending or terminating current contracts, withholding of progress payments, and debarment. Final determinations on violations are enforceable through the courts.

Relation to state, local and other federal laws

OFCCP generally refers individual complaints to the Equal Employment Opportunities Commission for investigation and resolution. The Executive Order applies to State and local government entities which have contracts with the Federal government if the State or local government entity participates in work on or under the contract or subcontract. Unlike coverage of private sector employers, the government entity but not the government as a whole becomes subject to the Executive Order when it enters into the contract.

Wage, Hour and Fringe Benefit Standards for Construction Contracts (DOL)

Who is covered

The Davis-Bacon and related Acts (40 USC §276a; 29 CFR 1, 3, 5, 6 and 7) are applicable to contractors and subcontractors performing on federally funded or assisted contracts in excess of $2,000 for the construction, alteration, or repair, including painting and decorating, of public buildings or public works. The Acts are administered and enforced by the Department of Labor's Employment Standards Administration, Wage and Hour Division.

Basic provisions/requirements

- The Act requires that all contractors and subcontractors performing on federal contracts, (and most contractors or subcontractors performing on federally assisted contracts under the Related Acts) in excess of $2,000 pay their laborers and mechanics not less than the wage rates and fringe benefits determined by the Secretary of Labor to be prevailing in the area for corresponding classes of laborers and mechanics employed on projects of a similar nature.

- Apprentices and trainees may be employed at less than the predetermined rates. Apprentices must be employed pursuant to an apprenticeship program registered with the Department of Labor or with a state apprenticeship agency recognized by the Department. Trainees must be employed pursuant to a training program certified by the Department.

- Contractors and subcontractors are also required, pursuant to the Contract Work Hours and Safety Standards Act, to pay employees one and one-half times their basic rate of pay for all hours worked on covered contract work over 40 in a workweek.

- Covered contractors and subcontractors are also required to pay employees weekly and submit weekly certified payroll records to the contracting agency.

- The Davis-Bacon Act is administered and enforced by the Employment Standards Administration's Wage and Hour Division.

Note: In a recent final rule (November 20, 2000), the Wage and Hour Division of the Employment Standards Administration adopted an amendment to the regulations that govern the employment of "helpers" on federally-financed and assisted construction contracts subject to the prevailing wage standards of the Davis-Bacon and Related Acts (DBRA).

Specifically, the document amends the regulations to incorporate the Wage and Hour Division's longstanding policy of recognizing helper classifications and wage rates only where their duties are clearly defined and distinct from those of journeyworker and laborer classifications in the area; the use of such helpers is an established prevailing practice in the area; and the term "helper" is not synonymous with "trainee" in an informal training program.

Penalties

Contractors or subcontractors who have been found to have disregarded their obligations to employees or have committed aggravated or willful violations while performing work on Davis-Bacon covered projects may be subject to contract termination and debarment from future contracts for up to three years. In addition, contract payments may be withheld in sufficient amounts to satisfy liabilities for unpaid wages and liquidated damages (resulting from overtime violations of the Contract Work Hours and Safety Standards Act).

Contractors and subcontractors may appeal determinations of violations and debarment to an administrative law judge. Appeals of administrative law judge decisions may be filed with the Administrative Review Board. Final determinations on violations may be appealed to and are enforceable through the courts.

Falsification of certified payroll records may subject a contractor or subcontractor to civil or criminal prosecution, the penalty for which may be fines and/or imprisonment.

Related Regulations for Construction

Relation to state, local and other federal laws

Since 1931, Congress has extended the Davis-Bacon prevailing wage requirements to some 60 related acts which provide federal assistance for construction through loans, grants, loan guarantees and insurance. These acts include by reference the requirements for payment of prevailing wages in accordance with the Davis-Bacon Act. Examples of the related acts are the Federal-Aid Highway Acts, the Housing and Community Development Act of 1974, and the Federal Water Pollution Control Act.

Kickbacks in Federally Funded Construction (DOL)

Who is covered

The Anti-Kickback section of the Copeland Act (18 USC §874 and 40 USC §276c; 29 CFR 3) applies to all contractors and subcontractors performing on any federally funded or assisted contract for the construction, prosecution, completion or repair of any public building or public work—except contracts for which the only Federal assistance is a loan guarantee. This provision applies even where the contract is not covered by a labor standards statute. The regulations pertaining to the Copeland Act payroll deductions and submission of the weekly statement of compliance apply only to contractors and subcontractors performing on federally funded contracts in excess of $2,000 and federally assisted contracts in excess of $2,000 that are subject to Federal wage standards. The Act is administered and enforced by the Department of Labor's Employment Standards Administration, Office of Federal Contract Compliance Programs.

Basic provisions/requirements

- The Anti-Kickback section of the Act precludes a contractor or subcontractor from inducing an employee—in any manner—to give up any part of his/her compensation to which he/she is entitled under his/her contract of employment.

- The Act and implementing regulations require a contractor and subcontractor to submit a weekly statement of the wages paid each employee performing on covered work during the preceding payroll period.

- The regulations also list payroll deductions that are permissible without the approval of the Secretary of Labor and those deductions that require consent of the Secretary of Labor.

- The Wage and Hour Division of the Employment Standards Administration enforces the provisions of the Act and implementing regulations.

Penalties

Any contractor or subcontractor who induces an employee working on a covered contract to give up any part of the compensation to which he/she is entitled is subject to a $5,000 fine, or imprisonment for up to 5 years, or both. The willful falsification of the statement of compliance may subject the employer to civil or criminal prosecution and may be cause for contract termination or debarment. Contractors may appeal determinations on debarment to an administrative law judge. Administrative law judge decisions may be appealed to the Administrative Review Board. Final determinations on debarment may be appealed to and are enforceable through the courts. Civil and criminal sanctions are pursued through the courts.

Key Word Index

	Page
Abatement verification	71
Abrasive grinding	29
Accident prevention	11, 24
Accident prevention signs and tags	24
Accident recordkeeping/reporting requirements	72
Administrative controls	14, 15, 18
Aerial lifts	33, 39, 47, 65
Americans With Disabilities Act	131
Annual Inspections	46
Annual summary	73
Arc welding	31
Asbestos	60, 117
Assured equipment grounding conductor program	33
Barricades	25, 27, 52
Body belts	44
Child Labor Provisions (DOL)	133
Citations	7, 70
Community Right to Know	127
Cold stress	113
Communication towers	93
Competent person	11, 26, 37, 38, 40, 45, 46, 52, 53, 55, 59, 60, 63
Compressed air	29
Compressed gases and cylinders	30, 31
Concrete and masonry construction	16, 29, 32, 42, 54
Confined spaces	12, 24, 58
Contractor safety/health requirements	11
Covers	12, 34, 35, 41, 44, 45
Cranes and derricks	40, 46, 50
Crystalline silica	77

	Page
Demolition	22, 55, 60
Disposal	27, 60, 63
Drinking water	13
Dusts	15, 21, 28
Egress	12, 51
Electrical	16, 20, 29, 32, 33, 35, 41, 47, 50
Emergency action plans	13
Employment Discrimination in Construction (DOL)	137
Engineering controls	14, 15, 18, 21, 61
Engineering survey	55
Environmental Protection Agency	117, 118, 122, 125, 127, 129
Excavations	50-53, 82
Exit markings	12
Exposure assessment	18, 19, 60-62
Extension cords (flexible cords)	33-35
Eye and face protection	13, 19, 20, 31
Eyewash facilities	13
Fabricated frame scaffolds	38, 39
Fair Labor Standards Act—Child Labor Provisions (DOL)	133
Fall protection	40-45, 54-56, 59
Fall protection for scaffolding	37, 38
Falling objects protection	20, 31, 38, 42, 45, 48, 51, 52
Family and Medical Leave Act (DOL)	135
Fire extinguishers	22-24, 47, 49
Fire prevention	22, 31
Fire protection	22, 24
First aid	13, 16
Flagmen	25, 103
Flammable and combustible liquids, substances, materials	12, 22-24, 28, 30, 31, 51

Key Word Index

	Page
Focused Inspection Initiative	84
Foot protection	20, 62
Forklift training	50
Forklifts	48, 50
Fueling/refueling	16, 23
Fumes	15, 21, 28
Gas welding	30, 31
Gases	12, 15, 21, 28
Gases, vapors, fumes, dusts, mists	15, 21, 28
General Duty Clause	69, 70
General safety and health provisions	11, 63
Ground fault circuit interrupters	33
Ground fault protection	33
Grounding/grounded conductors	29, 33-35, 47
Guarding, electrical	33, 35
Guarding, mechanical	28-30
Guardrail systems	36-38, 41-45
Hand tools	28, 29
Hazard communication	16, 17, 19
Hazardous atmospheres	51-53
Hazardous waste	28, 63, 129
Hazardous substances	12, 14, 51
Head protection	20, 62
Hearing conservation program	14
Hearing protection	20
Heat stress	110
Hoists/hoisting	26, 30, 41, 44, 46-48
Hoist area	25, 41
Holes	27, 41, 43
Housekeeping	12, 60, 63
Illumination	15, 16
Injuries, illnesses, and fatalities	12, 13, 72-75

	Page
Inspections (by employer)	11, 26, 40, 46-48, 52, 53
Inspections (by OSHA)	70
Jacks	48
Kickbacks in Federally Funded Construction (DOL)	141
Labels, markings, placards	15-17, 19, 32, 63
Ladder jack scaffolds	39
Ladders	21, 37, 39, 41, 43, 47, 51, 55-59
Lasers	15
Lead	18, 19, 79, 118
Lifelines	38, 44, 52
Limited access zones	54
Liquified petroleum gas (LPG)	23
Lockout/tagout	35, 67, 68
Machine guarding	28-30
Machinery and equipment	11, 29, 46-48, 65
Masonry construction	54
Material disposal	27, 55
Material handling equipment	25, 26
Material safety data sheets (MSDS)	16, 17, 19
Materials storage	15, 16, 22-25, 30, 31, 60
Means of egress	12, 51
Medical services and first aid	13, 16
Mists	15, 21, 28
Mobile scaffolds	39
Motor vehicles, mechanized equipment, and marine operations	48, 49
Multi-employer worksites	17
Noise exposure	14, 15, 20, 49
Nonionizing radiation	15
Occupational noise exposure	14, 15, 20, 49
Overhead power lines	37, 47, 49

Key Word Index

	Page
Personal fall arrest systems	38, 41, 42, 44
Personal protective equipment	12, 14, 20, 28, 29, 51, 66, 67
Portable ladders	37, 57-59
Positioning device systems	41
Posting of notice	68
Power tools	28, 29
Power transmission apparatus	30
Protective systems (shields, shoring, etc.)	52, 53
Pump jack scaffolds	39
Recording injuries, illnesses, fatalities	72-75
Reinforcing steel (rebar)	41, 54
Residential construction	42, 89
Respiratory protection	18, 20, 21, 51, 61
Rigging equipment for materials handling	26
Safety belts	21, 44, 55
Safety cans	22, 23
Safety monitoring systems	42, 44
Safety nets	21, 41-43, 54
Safety training and education	12
Sanitation	13-15
Scaffolding	21, 24, 36-40, 48, 54
Seat belts	49
Signaling (flagmen)	25, 103
Signs/tags	12, 19, 23, 27, 35, 62
Slings	26, 27, 48
Solvents	28
Stairways	37, 41, 47, 51, 55, 56, 59
Steel erection	41, 54, 91
Storage	15, 16, 22-25, 30, 31, 60
Stormwater	122

	Page
Suspended personnel platforms	36, 47
Synthetic slings	27
Taglines	55
Temporary electrical wiring	33
Temporary flooring	21, 54, 55
Temporary heating devices	24
Temporary lighting	33
Toilets	14, 16
Tools, hand and power	28, 29
Toxic materials	12
Training/instruction	11, 16, 19, 40, 45, 50, 59
Transmission/distribution lines and equipment	41, 47
Trenching, (see excavations)	
Tubular welded frame scaffolds	38
Ultraviolet radiation	108
Underground utilities	50, 51
Vapors	15, 21, 28
Ventilation	24, 31, 51
Wage, Hour and Fringe Benefits Standards for Construction Contracts (DOL)	139
Warning line systems	42, 44
Washing facilities	14, 19
Waste material disposal	27, 28, 63
Water	13, 21, 22, 50, 52
Welding and cutting	30, 32
Wetlands	125
Wire rope	26, 43, 46, 54
Woodworking tools	27, 29
Work platforms	65
Work zones	103